W9-AXI-873

A Dying Colonialism

Also Published by Grove Press

Black Skin, White Masks
The Wretched of the Earth

Frantz Fanon

A DYING COLONIALISM

Translated from the French by
Haakon Chevalier
With an Introduction by
Adolfo Gilly

GROVE PRESS, INC.
NEW YORK

First published as *Studies in a Dying Colonialism*

Originally published in France as *L' An Cinq de la Révolution Algérienne* © 1959 by François Maspero

First Evergreen Edition 1967
Third printing

Manufactured in the United States of America

Contents

Introduction

Revolution is mankind's way of life today. This is the age of revolution; the "age of indifference" is gone forever. But the latter age paved the way for today; for the great masses of mankind, while still suffering the greatest oppression and the greatest affronts to their dignity as human beings, never ceased to resist, to fight as well as they could, to live in combat. The combatant dignity of humanity was maintained in an unbreakable though not always visible line, in the depths of the life of the masses and in the uninterrupted fight—slandered, attacked, but alive in the very center of history—of little revolutionary vanguards bound to this profound human reality and to its socialist future, and not to the apparent omnipotence of great systems.

Today the great systems have died or are living in a state of crisis. And it is no longer the age of little vanguards. The whole of humanity has erupted violently, tumultuously onto the stage of history, taking its own destiny in its hands. Capitalism is under siege, surrounded by a global tide of revolution. And this revolution, still without a center, without a precise form, has its own laws, its own life and a depth of unity—accorded it by the same masses who create it, who live it, who inspire each other from across boundaries, give each other spirit and encouragement, and learn from their collective experiences.

This revolution is changing humanity. In the revolutionary struggle, the immense, oppressed masses of the colonies and semi-colonies feel that they are a part of life for the first time. Life acquires a sense, a transcendence, an object: to end exploitation, to govern themselves by and for themselves, to construct a way of life. The armed struggle breaks up the old routine life of the countryside and villages, excites, exalts, and opens wide the doors of the future. Liberation does not come as a gift from anybody; it is seized by the masses with their own hands. And by seizing it they themselves are transformed; confidence in their own strength soars, and they turn their energy and their experience to the tasks of building, governing, and deciding their own lives for themselves.

This is the climate in which the immense majority of mankind lives today in one way or another. Algeria has been, and continues to be, one of the great landmarks in this global battle. And Frantz Fanon's book bears witness to Algeria's role.

The book continues to have for the reader years afterwards the same freshness it had at the time it was written, because Fanon's main preoccupation was not to document the facts of exploitation, nor the sufferings of the people, nor the brutality of the imperialist oppressor. All this is demonstrated in passing. But his main interest has been to go to the essentials: the spirit of struggle, of opposition, of initiative of the Algerian masses; their infinite, multiform, interminable resistance; their daily heroism; their capacity to learn in weeks, in days, in minutes, all that was necessary for the struggle for liberation; their capacity and decision to make all the sacrifices and all the efforts, among which the greatest was not giving one's life in combat, perhaps, but changing one's daily life, one's routines, prejudices, and immemorial customs insofar as these were a hindrance to the revolutionary struggle.

Frantz Fanon died at 37, in December of 1961, days before the appearance of the first edition of *Les Damnés de la Terre.*[1] He was not a Marxist. But he was approaching Marxism through the same essential door which for many "Marxist" officials and diplomats is closed with seven keys: his concern with what the masses do and say and think, and his belief that it is the masses, and not leaders nor systems, who in the final analysis make and determine history. This is the dominant line of all of Marx's analyses of historical events, whether in his articles on

[1] Published in English under the title *The Wretched of the Earth,* New York, 1965.

revolution and counter-revolution in Spain, or in his moving pages on the centuries-old struggle of the Sicilian people, a struggle which has forged the character, the pride, and the silence of Sicily and which is at the root of its present and its future.

The masses resist and fight in a thousand ways, not only with arms in hand. These means include violence because in a world where oppression is maintained by violence from above, it is only possible to liquidate it with violence from below. Ultimately, once the struggle reaches a certain point, arms in hand are indispensable.

On November 1, 1954, a small group of Algerian leaders launched an armed struggle, breaking with a whole pattern of negotiation and procrastination established by the old leaders. In a very short time, they had the entire population behind them. The decision to take arms did not spring full-blown from the heads of this handful of leaders. They simply interpreted what was already there in the population as a whole. And the people, in turn, were influenced by revolutions in the rest of the world. In 1949 China tipped decisively and definitively the balance of world power in favor of revolution. In 1951 she risked her own existence to send hundreds of thousands of volunteers to support the Korean revolution. In 1954, Dien Bien Phu was a culminating disaster, marking the end of French domination in Indo-China. This was the signal for Algeria to launch her struggle. And in 1960-1961, the defeat of French imperialism in Algeria unleashed the great tide of African revolution.

The revolutionaries of Zanzibar took advantage of this uninterrupted chain of revolutionary struggles to realize one of the greatest deeds of the epoch: storming the center of power with a small nucleus, they expelled imperialism from a backward country with only 300,000 inhabitants. They took the road of socialist revolution, arms in hand, with no other support than the determination of the masses of Zanzibar—barefoot, poor, illiterate, armed as well as they could manage—and their own revolutionary courage.

Algeria was prepared by the incessant waves of revolution that inundated the world from 1943 onwards, and in its turn opened the gates to Zanzibar, to the Congo, Mali, Portuguese Guinea. The Algerian revolution shares with the revolutions that preceded it and with those that are continuing it, certain essential features which can be summed up in the words "mass participation."

The women, the family, the children, the aged—everybody participates. The double oppression, social and sexual, of the woman cracks and is finally shattered; and its essential nature as the social oppression of the family as a whole is revealed. It is simply that its weakest parts—the children, the elderly, the women—must bear the most exaggerated forms of oppression. But in the revolutionary struggle, the relative weakness, the apparent defenselessness of these groups disappear. What was formerly a disadvantage becomes an advantage for the revolution. The old man or woman who walks with halting steps past the military patrol, the timid woman hiding behind a veil, the innocent-faced child do not seem to the enemy to be dangers or threats. So they can pass arms, information, medicine. They can prepare surprise attacks, serve as guides and sentries. They can even take up arms themselves. Every sort of cunning is a legitimate weapon to use against the enemy—and an embattled population is not composed solely of men but also of women, children, and old people.

This is true not only in Algeria or in armed struggle. The decision of the men never comes alone; it is never isolated. It is supported by the decision of the whole family, of the whole population, united for a common objective. When the striking worker occupies the factory, or makes a decision in a union meeting to stick to the struggle against all odds, it is not he alone who decides. Behind him are his wife, his children, his parents, the entire family supporting him, intervening and deciding with him. This is what happens in Bolivia in the great miners' strikes; it happens in Argentina in the general strikes; it happened in the great struggles of the North American proletariat, as reflected, for example, in the film *The Salt of the Earth.*

It is in this kind of struggle that the woman stands firm in her own strength, throws all the energy she has accumulated during centuries of oppression, her infinite capacity to resist, her courage. It is in this kind of struggle that family relations change and the woman prepares for her role in the society that is being built. She also prepares for it in battle. This is what Fanon describes, and what he describes is no different from what the Chinese and the Cuban women did. The Algerian woman who carries arms or who participates directly in combat is like the wife of the Bolivian miner who takes up arms to defend the occupied mines or who keeps watch, gun in hand and dynamite at her waist, over the hostages taken by the miners to be exchanged for the liberty of their own imprisoned leaders. She is like the Guatemalan peasant woman who diverts the attention of the army at the cost of her own life, to cover the retreat of a guerrilla patrol in which her son, or her husband, or simply her neighbor is marching. This is the kind of life that is being lived and the kind of revolution that humanity is passing through today. And Fanon shows how, after it is over, the place of women can never again be the same as it was before. Women, like the proletariat, can only liberate themselves by liberating all other oppressed strata and sectors of the society, and by acting together with them.

To describe a revolution one doesn't have to describe armed actions. These are inevitable, but what defines and decides any revolution is the social struggle of the masses, supported by armed actions. Fanon shows that this was the Algerian way. The guerrillas in the mountains, the army of liberation, did not defeat the French army militarily: it was the whole population supported by the guerrilla army which defeated and destroyed the imperialist enemy as a social force. For each Algerian soldier who died, says Fanon, ten civilians died. This indicates the mass character of the struggle. But it also indicates the complete impotence of an army, of modern weapons, and of all the tactics of powerful nations when it comes to defeating an embattled people with infinite initiative and inexhaustible heroism, a people capable of constant surprises and enormous tenacity. All mass struggles develop these features. The armed combatants, the guerrilla fighters, are only centers of support, of encouragement, of organization for this massive movement that reaches into every nook and cranny of the population.

For this reason, the power of each guerrilla fighter does not rest simply in himself, his weapon, and his army unit. He is the incarnation of the will of the people to struggle, of the resistance, of the anonymous and innumerable ways in which the people seek to harass and liquidate the oppressor and refuse to collaborate with him. This is the only "magic" the guerrillas have—that they are the representatives of a social force immensely superior to their own numbers and fire power, a social force that constantly encircles, attacks, and intimidates the enemy.

The capitalist and imperialist armies can go on dozens of mopping-up operations and even achieve some relative successes, militarily speaking. But after the guerrillas have taken root to a certain point, they can no longer be liquidated. For the guerrillas have already become a way of life for the population, a part of its existence, and they will be renewed, reborn, and will go forward whatever the situation or the apparent power of the enemy. The French army announced time after time the "final offensive" and "the last quarter hour." It was ruined, defeated—as before it had been defeated in Indo-China. It wasn't simply the guerrilla arms that routed the French, but the constant action, the constant struggle of the entire population who fought them even to the point of listening to the radio and re-inventing the news, as the Guatemalan and Colombian peasants do today.

For the radio is an instrument of mass struggle. The counterrevolutionary forces believe they have discovered this also, and they use "The Voice of America" in Latin America as yesterday "Radio Alger" was used in Algeria. But the radio is an instrument of struggle only when what it says corresponds to what the masses feel and want. Then they accept it, take it, rely on it to further their cause. And when they cannot hear what it says, why they invent what it says—to the greater glory of the revolution. In contrast, the counter-revolutionary radio is not listened to; its voice is lost in a complete vacuum.

The Algerian people accepted the radio when it ceased to be an instrument of the enemy and was useful for the revolution. In the same way the Cuban people accepted literacy and achieved it in a year when this became a goal of the revolution, when they saw it was tied to their own concrete interests and not to those of capitalist governments. The transistor radio has been transformed into a revolutionary implement as powerful as the gun. In the mountains of Guatemala and Colombia, the peasants listen to Radio Havana or Radio Peking and live the life of the world revolution.

In Bolivia the miners have more than transistor radios. The principal mineworkers' unions have their own radio transmitters. And the miners' radios are one of the great instruments of progress in Bolivia. When there is an attempt on the part of the press and official radio to hide the fact of a miners' strike by not reporting it, the miners' radios inform all of Bolivia—and beyond, for they are short-wave transmitters that can be heard as far away as Peru and Uruguay. When the army tries to isolate one mining district from another, the miners' radios communicate with each other and unite the different union locals. Via the radio the union members at one mine discuss agreements and situations with those at another. Via the radio, union propaganda is disseminated, as well as the programs and decisions adopted at meetings, calls to action, and proclamations. Via their radios the mineworkers' militia is called together or the advances of the army are announced. Via the radio came the announcement of the defeat of the Bolivian army at the hands of the mineworkers' militia in Sora Sora at the end of 1964. And because the miners have radio transmitters, the peasants acquire transistor radios in order to listen to them.

As in Algeria, the Bolivian miners defend their radio transmitters as part of their collective existence. Many unions have bought their transmitter with voluntary contributions of a day's, two days' and even three days' wages per month from all the workers in the mine. The Bolivian miner earns $20 to $40 per month. One must consider his standard of living in order to understand what it means for him to give up a day's or two days' wages each month so that the union can get its radio. But then, the collective pride: "Our union has a radio, too!" When the government or the police have wished to silence or take by assault such a radio (officially they are prohibited, the government having declared them illegal—but in the mining districts the union and not the government commands) the response has been explosive. In Huanuni the miners took back their radio by mobilizing their militia and in retaliation they took over the municipal radio of the district as well, which from then on was controlled by the miners. Though they didn't know it, Bolivian miners and Algerian masses were united in a single action for a single end. In this way, and not through books, business deals, or international assemblies is the present unity of humanity being forged and constructed.

Frantz Fanon tells how modern medical techniques, when they were brought in by imperialism, were resisted and rejected by the Algerian population—"ignorant, obstinate, backward" according to the cultured imperialists who were baffled by this rejection. But these same techniques were accepted with dizzying haste when the revolution adopted them. Culture, like truth, is concrete. And for the masses the most elevated form of culture, that is to say, of progress, is to resist imperialist domination and penetration, although this might come wrapped up in valid forms of "culture" or "civilization." The Algerians kept their women behind veils, rejected the doctors, would not accept the radio. But they were not backward. In their way, they were defending civilization as well as they were able. Civilization, for them, meant first of all to resist imperialism and second to cast it into the sea at whatever cost. And they were right.

One morning, from the home of the Bolivian miner who was giving me lodging—a home measuring two meters by three, the walls and floor of which were of earth, and which housed his wife and child as well—I saw that there was an ambulance at the corner from the Inter-American Health Service. It was giving free vaccinations against smallpox. I asked my host why he didn't send his son to be vaccinated. And he answered, "Are you crazy? Who knows what kind of filth these *gringos* are injecting, in order to turn us Bolivians into idiots so they can exploit us better?" Thus are the "Alliances for Progress" received. Basically, the miner was right. For in his way he was defending something that was much more important to him than a vaccination.

But the revolution triumphs and everything changes. A devouring thirst for knowledge invades the entire population, whether in the new nation or in the liberated territories of a nation in revolt. And because of this, Fanon states: "The people who take their destiny into their own hands assimilate the most modern forms of technology at an extraordinary rate." As in China, in Cuba, in Korea, as with all the oppressed peoples of Latin America, of Asia, of Africa, the revolution is civilization. And also in Portugal, in Spain, in Greece, and in the south of Italy and beyond.

This book of Fanon covers a particularly crucial period in the Algerian revolution. It was during the first five years—when the people were fighting virtually alone, almost without outside help—that the people decided once and for all to stand firm and laid the foundations for their triumph. Algeria was never completely alone. She had the support of the masses of the Arab countries, who secured the support of their governments—many of which had been dragging their feet on the issue. She had the support of the peoples of the world, who followed her fight very closely. But she was alone in material means, in material support. She had no support from the USSR, and support from China came only in 1959. And in the first years she had to break by means of her own heroism the wall of silence and slander that was being erected not only by the enemy but also by those who later declared themselves to be Algeria's friends.

People never forget the past—or what the past teaches that is of importance for the future. The Algerian people have not forgotten that the French Communist Party, at the beginning of the armed revolution in Algeria, denounced it as a "nationalist and reactionary" movement. And for a long time the Party maintained this position or kept aloof while continuing to insist that Algeria was part of France. Neither have the people forgotten that the Algerian Communist Party followed the line of the French Party, although many individual Communists cast their lot with the revolution. Nor have they forgotten those who, during this period, gave lip service to the revolution while in practice supporting Messali Hadj, an instrument of French imperialism who called himself a "socialist" in order to combat the revolutionary mass movement from within Algeria itself. The people haven't forgotten any of this, because they are practical and they scorn forever those who out of selfishness or criminal blindness fought the liberation movement, denounced it, or betrayed it, meanwhile calling themselves "revolutionaries" or "Communists" or "socialists." Such people, once the collective experience of the masses is accomplished, are never again influential, no matter what money or means they may have at their disposal.

But just as they have not forgotten this, the Algerian people have not forgotten either that the sympathy of the masses of the world was embodied in hundreds of thousands of men of flesh and bone who went beyond or ignored the pacifist politics of the French Communist Party and the diplomatic considerations that kept Khrushchev from giving arms to Algeria and made him appear instead to be friendly with a French government in open imperialist warfare against the Algerian people. As Fanon points out, these hundreds of thousands, in France and in Algeria itself, supported Algeria without being Algerians, participated in her struggle, and risked their lives for the Algerian revolution.

These men were not only Frenchmen or Arabs; they were also Spaniards, Italians, Greeks—the entire Mediterranean supported an Algeria in arms. And from beyond came Englishmen, Dutchmen, Belgians, Germans, Latin Americans. Like every great revolution, the Algerian revolution attracted men from all over the world, and received them as its own. Those who went not only made their contribution to the struggle of that moment but, by the simple fact of their presence in the struggle for liberation, helped to model the future image of the Algeria that is being built today, to move her in the direction of international socialism. As individuals or as groups, they symbolized concretely the will to support the revolution of much broader groups who could find no way to participate directly.

An important feature of Fanon's book is that he doesn't dwell on the torture, the pain, and the sufferings of the Algerian people; rather, he emphasizes their life and inner strength. Certainly he tells about tortures, but he doesn't stop there. And, above all, he doesn't want to arouse compassion for the Algerian people, but confidence in their strength. In this he disassociated himself from numerous "defenders" of the revolution—in Algeria or elsewhere—who assumed a protective and compassionate tone and invited us to take pity on an embattled people and to cease the atrocities.

This was a characteristic of a good many European "friends" of the Algerian revolution, as it is today of many "friends" of the Vietnamese revolution. They approached the Algerians with a terribly paternalistic air to sympathize with their sufferings. In any struggling people this kind of "help" arouses an immediate and instinctive rejection, because they feel that it is the "pacifist" form of the old colonialism and they feel that it damages the innermost source of their fighting power—their faith in their own strength, their confidence in their ultimate superiority over the imperialist enemy. The Algerians rejected all paternalistic defenders, as the Vietnamese reject them today. The images of destruction, of death, of horror, inspire aversion in the combatant, because he doesn't confront them with pity but with a gun in hand. "Instead of pitying us and being horrified by the atrocities of imperialism, better fight against it in your own country as we do in ours," said the Algerians, and say other colonial peoples today to their new pacifist protectors. "That is the best way to help us and to put an end to the atrocities."

The essence of revolution is not the struggle for bread; it is the struggle for human dignity. Certainly this includes bread. And at the base of any revolutionary situation are economic conditions. But beyond a certain point of development, on this same basis, it is more important for a people to have guns in hand than to eat more than the year before. This is demonstrated by all revolutions. And to the degree that the boundaries of the revolution are extended and become one with those of the globe itself, immediate economic conditions are secondary to the movement of the masses to liquidate all forms of oppression and govern themselves by and for themselves. As a result of this desire for liberation and human dignity, the dominating feature of humanity today, people accept and assume the material sacrifices of years which any revolution requires, because they feel that thus they live a new life, a better life, and that for the first time they are really living their *own* lives.

"The colonized person, who in this respect is like the men in underdeveloped countries or the disinherited in all parts of the world, perceives life not as a flowering or a development of an essential productiveness, but as a permanent struggle against an omnipresent death. This ever-menacing death is experienced as endemic famine, unemployment, a high mortality rate, an inferiority complex and the absence of any hope for the future," says Frantz Fanon.

The revolution ends all that; the source of human dignity, it is preparing humanity, through its transformation in the revolution, for the construction of socialism. Without this transformation there will be no material base for the building of socialism. I say *material* advisedly since it is not only the means of production which are material, but also the accumulated experience in the heads, hearts, and hands of men.

For this reason Fanon closes his book with these words: "The revolution in depth, the true one, precisely because it changes man and renews society, has reached an advanced stage. This oxygen which creates and shapes a new humanity—this, too, is the Algerian Revolution." And it is also, one must add today, the *socialist* revolution which is advancing in Algeria.

If the revolution changes a people in this way—if it is capable of illuminating and influencing Europe and Africa as it has been doing, this is because it is part of a global process which knows no boundaries. If, as an example, the Algerians were able to cast out French imperialism, it was not only by the heroism of their struggle but also because in one way or another, and despite the reformist character of their official instructions, French workers continued to resist French capitalism, to threaten it, to undermine it from within. They didn't have the means to do more, but without their presence French imperialism would have felt strong enough to resist in Algeria for a longer time.

At the same time, the Algerian victory demonstrated how a revolution can stand firm and triumph without a great deal of outside support, securing or even making its own weapons, if it is capable of uniting the masses of the country in the struggle for liberation. There is no doubt that Algeria, like every revolutionary process in the world, has made its powerful influence felt even inside the Soviet Union. The Soviet people know that it was only at the last minute that their government lent its support to Algeria. Today they have drawn their conclusions, and one of them is that Khrushchev is no more. Other conclusions will come later; they are slowly ripening inside the Soviet Union. For it is certainly obvious that, if in Algeria the masses had and have the inner life of their own that Fanon describes, the same life with the same aims exists in the Soviet Union, although it is expressed in a different form. And just as the Algerian is united with the Cuban, the Bolivian, the Congolese, through certain obvious acts carried out in common, he is also united with the Soviet and the Chinese citizen. The immediate course of history will show the development of this union more and more clearly through more and more palpable deeds.

And the Algerian is also united with the American. If Algeria was once alone, today this is no longer possible. Khrushchev wanted to ignore Vietnam—and he fell. Vietnam is today the center of the global struggle between revolution and counter-revolution. In a certain sense, it is today what Algeria was during that fifth year of the revolution in 1959. But what a difference! Today the war in Vietnam involves immense powers. The Soviet population, the Chinese population follow hour by hour what is happening in Vietnam, and there cannot be the slightest doubt that they are pressuring for intervention. But the American population is following these events, too. And although their feelings are not clear, and even still terribly confused, one cannot doubt either that the dominant line of pressure, however it may be expressed, is to restrain their own leaders from unleashing a world war. Even in this contradictory form of fears, vacillations, and doubts in the face of the world situation—which did not exist during the war against the Axis powers—the pressure of the world revolution is weighing on the United States. This pressure is building up to produce a more positive response on the part of the student movements—still small but very explicit—opposing American intervention in Vietnam. Never, in any country, does a significant mass of students represent only themselves; they represent a whole sector of the population that has not yet decided to express itself. This is valid for the Soviet Union as well as for the United States.

To be sure, it is not student demonstrations that will decide whether or not a major war will be launched. The balance of forces is immensely more complex and in the end the decisive buttons are controlled by only a few persons beyond all control, who may feel compelled to act in the face of a situation they consider desperate for their own survival: the imminent threat that in a particular moment the loss of Vietnam would bring in its wake the loss of all Asia may be such a situation.

But the great value of Fanon's descriptions of the conduct of the masses is in underlining the importance of their inner life, their private discussions, their resistance, their seemingly indirect actions. All this exists among all the peoples of the world. It is on this deep level that the future—which will later on seem to burst suddenly and without warning into bloom—is being prepared. The same thing happens in the United States. Resistance to the war in Vietnam, however weak it may seem in comparison with the apparent omnipotence of the imperialist apparatus, must be understood as a highly important symptom of what is gestating in the still unconscious depths of broad segments of the population. The United States is not isolated by any *cordon sanitaire* from the revolution which is engulfing mankind, and each aggressive step that its government takes along the road of counter-revolution inevitably awakens opposing forces within the country.

It is worth the trouble to analyze the testimony of Fanon because it illustrates how, in the midst of the worst disasters, the masses find the means of reorganizing themselves and continuing their existence when they have a common objective. Systems cannot do this. Nations fall, armies collapse, businesses close or are expropriated, colonists flee, a city is destroyed by bombardment. But the masses go on living; they tenaciously recreate themselves, bury their dead, and go forward. It is worth the trouble to analyze Fanon, for the life of humanity today, as in Algeria, is preparing the life of tomorrow. The desire, the collective decision for social liberation is so rooted in the very life of all mankind that it is as much a part of their existence as is the earth and the air. There is no power, no conventional or atomic weapon that can destroy it. All the rest may disappear—nations, enterprises, cities. That, no.

This idea is at the bottom of the Chinese strategy against atomic war. And it is also present in the strategy of the Soviet army, one of whose chiefs recently referred to the possible war as "a popular rising of the masses" and described the means being developed for reorganizing the life of the country in case of an atomic attack.

It is a fact that a people who went through the Algerian war do not feel intimidated by the atomic menace. Nor do the people who are living through the war in Vietnam. Nor even do those who, without experiencing actual warfare, live lives which are "a permanent struggle against an omnipresent death," as Fanon says. And it is easy to imagine that if one day the transistor radio of a Bolivian miner, or a Colombian peasant, or an Algerian *fellah* tells them that Moscow and Peking have been destroyed by atomic bombs, they will rise up furiously and instantaneously to destroy in turn all that which represents their enemies. And if in the same moment they are also told that, on the other side, New York has disappeared from the map, their strength will be multiplied because they will see that their enemies no longer have any support, and they will feel that an immense weight has been lifted from their shoulders. The testimony of Fanon—and how much distance has been covered since then!—should make us reflect that humanity, once it has reached such a degree of decision and collective conscience, cannot be destroyed by war, whatever may be the immeasurable damage war can wreak.

Perhaps this thesis is not very inspiring for a resident of New York. But it was inspiring for the Cubans in 1962 when they faced the imminent prospect of atomic destruction. On the 27th of October few people in Havana doubted that that afternoon they would undergo an atomic attack. Few had illusions about their chances. "They're going to wipe us out on the spot." But nobody was afraid or wavered. It was impressive, moving, this collective security. Cuba felt herself to be part of humanity. The entire population felt like the soldier who knows that, though the next skirmish will surely cost him his life, he must not flinch but must help prepare the way for the triumph of his friends. To the end Cuba was able to take her own destiny in hand, and she won. If in that moment she had vacillated, begged for a truce or fallen back, she would have lost, been invaded. Thus her decision was part of the strength that made the enemy draw back. "We'd rather have them kill us all than go back to the old life." This is what the Cuban said, what the Algerian said in his moment of decision, what the Chinese and the Vietnamese are saying. This very decision makes any threat ineffective and at the same time unites the destiny of the individual and the collectivity with that of humankind. The destiny of humankind is today found in revolution, one of whose stages is described from within by Fanon in this book.

Only by becoming a part of this worldwide revolution can the resident of New York take his human destiny upon his shoulders. Only thus will he find the door to the future, and only thus can his action be effective. Because this action rests not on humanitarian abstractions but on the real life of human beings today—in Algeria, Vietnam, the Congo, China, Indonesia, all of Latin America.

When the immense majority of humanity is living through these problems and these experiences, when the real life, the real future of thousands of millions is modelled on this revolutionary life, when humanity is taking its destiny in its hands in this way, it is pure charlatanism to talk of such things as a "cybernetic revolution." It is human beings—not systems, machines or weapons—who decide their own lives. To ignore this is to isolate a small segment of humanity, the population of the United States, from the life, the problems, and the changes that the immense majority of humanity is experiencing. It is to isolate this segment from the future and from life and to shut it up inside a provincial and pragmatic narrowness. It is the people of Algeria and Vietnam, not the Univacs nor the New York Stock Exchange who, in the final analysis, decide the future and who, together with the American people, will decide tomorrow what to do with the Univacs and with the vast technology which will belong to them.

Zanzibar, in an even more decisive form than Cuba, has demonstrated that today any revolution against imperialism cannot but lead the way to socialism. There is no anti-imperialist revolution in any colonial country that does not mean overthrowing capitalism at the same time. Algeria is another proof. And in this socialist objective the revolutions in the colonies today find the link which joins them to the coming American revolution. For this reason, any action that unites a segment of the American population, no matter how small it may seem, with the global revolution, represents and introduces in the United States an immense strength, in the same way that the Algerian combatant represented not only the fire power of his gun, but the constant and powerful action of an entire people.

This book by Fanon testifies not so much to the death of colonialism as to the life of the masses in this age of revolution. It continues to be today, in the still underdeveloped countries, a clarion call to make common cause, without reservations or limitations, with those masses, to become a part of their struggles, and above all to feel and understand as their own the tremendous strength of a united people. This means, really, to submit oneself to the profundity of the inner life—real, not apparent—of one's own people, to understand the signs and symptoms of the immediate future that will come out of those depths and not out of the superficial remnants of a dead past which still seems, but only seems, to control the future. In reality, Fanon is calling us all to prepare our place in this revolution that is challenging, transforming, and uniting all of humanity.

Adolfo Gilly

April, 1965

Postscript

In a small section of the city of Santo Domingo, Dominican people in arms are resisting the military invasion by American troops. Men, women, children, workers, soldiers, students, enclosed in a scant two square kilometers, without supplies, with-

out effective outside support—from Russia or anybody else—are resisting the greatest military power of the capitalist world. That power cannot advance, although it has the military force to wipe out this zone in less than an hour. Who and what is containing it? What is the force that is animating the Dominicans? The people in these two square kilometers are not alone. The entire Dominican population is expressing itself through these armed civilians in these few blocks. But the three and a half million Dominicans are not alone either. The force of the worldwide revolution, which sustained Algeria and is sustaining Zanzibar, has found a point of support in the armed population of Santo Domingo. These people, without declarations, without grand gestures, but simply by resisting with arms in hand, are representing that revolution day by day. They are the greatest symbol of human dignity.

Everything that yesterday permitted the Algerians to resist and conquer, is today being expressed by the Dominican people. If the Dominicans are able to resist in this way, this means that no revolutionary force or tendency, no matter how small it may seem, is alone or isolated if it knows how to represent, in its policies, its acts, and its life, this immense force that is transforming the world. In contrast, alone and isolated are those who, with great power and means, wish to brake this force or refuse to support the Dominicans with more than declarations. The Dominican crisis, like the Sino-Soviet and the Algerian crises, is indicating in its way that the profound reality of the revolutionary transformation is fighting to express itself openly and to do away with external appearances perpetuated from the past. The new content is creating cracks in the old forms which are trying to stifle it.

Tomorrow there will be no more arms. Today arms in the hands of a people change the deepest recesses of their lives. This introduction was already written when the military junta that governs Bolivia set out to snatch the arms, the radios, the workers' control from the miners, workers, and peasants of

Bolivia. The junta could advance and strike because the leadership fled at the first heavy attack. But the miners and workers resisted. More than ten days they fought with arms in hand, and carried out a general strike without centralized leadership and under enormous handicaps. The military junta, assassinating hundreds of people, was able to occupy the mines, take over the unions and the miners' radios, because there was no leadership to unite the workers and the popular forces which together would have been able to rout the junta. But the junta could not and will not be able to reach its essential objective: the recovery of the arms held by the miners and peasants. The army advanced, but the arms were hidden. Nobody responded to the invitation to turn over their guns. Without leadership the defeat was inevitable and the miners had to retreat. But they were not broken: proof—the hidden arms. Nobody hides a weapon—at the risk of death or of the loss of his wages, which in Bolivia is almost the same thing—if it is not in order to continue the resistance, if he is not already, by this act alone, continuing the battle.

The militias, the unions, and the revolution changed forever the Bolivian people, and this fact no military junta can erase. On the contrary, the permanent dynamism of the worldwide revolution will continue to find support within Bolivia. It will help to regroup forces, as today it is helping the Dominicans to resist, and to take the direction indicated by these forces, which is to wipe out the military junta and its social system and not simply to negotiate with it. For the old leadership's politics of negotiation simply led to dispersal and flight.

A single line unites Santo Domingo, Vietnam, Bolivia, Algeria: they are expressions of a single revolution that embraces the world. And from the moment when their peoples succeeded in taking their destiny in their hands by force of arms, nothing and nobody could make them retreat. With difficulty and through crises and conflicts like the Sino-Soviet and the Algerian ones, but stubbornly and inexorably nevertheless, they are making emerge the vanguards and the directions that represent the revolutionary stage of humanity, and they are preparing by their program and methods the advances and the socialist decisions for which humanity is already prepared.

Adolfo Gilly[2]

June, 1965

---

[2] Adolfo Gilly is an Argentine journalist who writes for several publications in Latin America, Italy, France and the United States. He is the author of the MR Press book, *Inside the Cuban Revolution.* This introduction was translated from the Spanish by Nell Salm.

Preface

The Algerian war will soon be entering its sixth year. No one among us in November 1954, no one in the world, suspected that after sixty months of fighting, French colonialism would still not have released its clutch and heeded the voice of the Algerian people.

Five years of struggle have brought no political change. The French authorities continue to proclaim Algeria to be French.

This war has mobilized the whole population, has driven them to draw upon their entire reserves and their most hidden resources. The Algerian people have given themselves no respite, for the colonialism against which they are pitted has allowed them none.

The Algerian war—the most hallucinatory war that any people has ever waged to smash colonial aggression. Its adversaries like to claim that the men who lead the Algerian Revolution are impelled by a thirst for blood. The democrats who were sympathetic to it repeat, for their part, that it has made mistakes.

It has in fact happened that Algerian citizens have violated the directives of the commanding bodies, and that things that should have been avoided have transpired on the national soil. Almost always, incidentally, these concerned Algerian citizens.

But what has the Revolution done in such cases? Has it eluded its responsibilities? Has it not penalized those whose acts threatened to compromise the truth of the combat we were waging? Has not Mr. Ferhat Abbas, president of the council of the G.P.R.A.[1], publicly announced the sometimes capital measures taken by the leadership of the Revolution?

[1] G.P.R.A.—*Gouvernement Provisoire de la République Algérienne,* the provisional government of the Algerian Republic. (Translator's note)

And yet what is psychologically more understandable than these sudden acts of violence against traitors and war criminals? The men who fought in the First French Army campaign had been revolted by the self-appointed dispensers of justice among their fellow-soldiers who shot at collaborators. Those who had recaptured the Isle of Elba, who had fought the campaign of Italy and had participated in the landing at Toulon were outraged by such fratricidal, illegal and often shamefully conducted settlings of accounts. Yet we do not remember any conviction of French guerrillas for summary executions preceded by tortures of unarmed citizens.

The National Liberation Front, at the time when the people were undergoing the most massive assaults of colonialism, did not hesitate to prohibit certain forms of action and constantly to remind the fighting units of the international laws of war. In a war of liberation, the colonized people must win, but they must do so cleanly, without "barbarity." The European nation that practices torture is a blighted nation, unfaithful to its history. The underdeveloped nation that practices torture thereby confirms its nature, plays the role of an underdeveloped people. If it does not wish to be morally condemned by the "Western nations," an underdeveloped nation is obliged to practice fair play, even while its adversary ventures, with a clear conscience, into the unlimited exploration of new means of terror.

An underdeveloped people must prove, by its fighting power, its ability to set itself up as a nation, and by the purity of every one of its acts, that it is, even to the smallest detail, the most lucid, the most self-controlled people. But this is all very difficult.

Whereas in the region of Mascara, exactly six months ago, more than thirty combatants—encircled and having exhausted their ammunition, after having fought with rocks—were taken prisoner and executed before the village, an Algerian doctor in another section detached a military mission from the frontier in order to bring back in haste medicine urgently needed to treat the ailment of a French prisoner. In the course of the journey two Algerian fighters were killed. On other occasions soldiers have been assigned to engage in a diversion maneuver to enable a group of prisoners to reach the regional command post unharmed.

The French ministers Lacoste and Soustelle have published photographs with a view to sullying our cause. Some of these photographs show things done by members of our Revolution. But there are other photographs that show some of the thousands of crimes of which the Bellounis and the *harkis*[2] armed by the French Army have themselves been guilty. Finally and above all, there are those tens of thousands of Algerian men and women who have been and continue to be victims of the French troops.

No, it is not true that the Revolution has gone to the lengths to which colonialism has gone.

But we do not on this account justify the immediate reactions of our compatriots. We understand them, but we can neither excuse them nor reject them.

Because we want a democratic and a renovated Algeria, because we believe one cannot rise and liberate oneself in one area and sink in another, we condemn, with pain in our hearts, those brothers who have flung themselves into revolutionary action with the almost physiological brutality that centuries of oppression give rise to and feed.

The people who condemn us or who blame us for these dark aspects of the Revolution know nothing of the terrible problem faced by the chief who must take disciplinary action against a patriot guilty, for example, of having killed a notorious traitor—or, worse, a woman or child—without having received orders to do so. This man who must be judged in the absence of a code, of any law, only by the conscience that each one has of what is allowable and what is forbidden, may not be a new man in the combat group. He may have given, over a period of months, unmistakable proofs of abnegation, of patriotism, of courage. Yet

[2] Bellouni—an F.L.N. leader who went over to the French. *Harki*—an Arab militiaman in the service of the French. (Translator's note)

he must be judged. The chief, the local representative of the ruling body, must apply the directives. He must sometimes be the accuser, the other members of the unit having been unwilling to accuse this brother before the revolutionary court.

It is not easy to conduct, with a minimum of errors, the struggle of a people, sorely tried by a hundred and thirty years of domination, against an enemy as determined and as ferocious as French colonialism.

Mrs. Christian Lilliestierna, the Swedish newspaperwoman, talked in a camp with some of the thousands of Algerian refugees. Here is an extract from her report:

> The next in the line was a boy of seven marked by deep wounds made by a steel wire with which he had been bound while French soldiers mistreated and killed his parents and his sisters. A lieutenant had forcefully kept the boy's eyes open, so that he would see and remember this for a long time. . . .
>
> This child was carried by his grandfather for five days and five nights before reaching the camp.
>
> The child said: "There is only one thing I want: to be able to cut a French soldier up into small pieces, tiny pieces!"

Does anyone think it is easy to make this child of seven forget both the murder of his family and his enormous vengeance? Is this orphaned child growing up in an apocalyptic atmosphere the sole message that French democracy will leave?

No one thought that France would defend foot by foot this shameless colonialism for five years, a colonialism which is matched, on the continent, by its homologue in South Africa. Nor did anyone suspect that the Algerian people would make its place in history with such intensity.

Nor must we delude ourselves. The rising generations are neither more flexible nor more tired than those who launched the struggle. There is, on the contrary, a hardening, a determination to be equal to the historical challenge, a determination, too, not to make light of hundreds of thousands of victims. And there is also an exact appraisal of the dimensions of the conflict, of the friendships and the solidarities, of the interests and the contradictions of the colonialist universe.

"Having a gun, being a member of the National Army of Liberation, is the only chance the Algerian still has of giving a meaning to his death. Life under the domination has long been devoid of meaning. . . ."

Such statements, when they are made by members of the Algerian government, are not the expression of an error of judgment or of a "to-the-bitter-end" attitude. They are the plain recognition of the truth.

There is in Algeria, as the Algerian people see it, an irreversible stituation. French colonialism itself has recognized it, and it attempts, anarchically, to tag along behind the historic movement. In the French National Assembly eighty Algerian deputies have seats. But today this serves no purpose.

The single college[8] has been accepted by the extremists of the domination, but in 1959 this appears ludicrous, in view of the extraordinary dimensions assumed by the Algerian national consciousness. Question any woman or any man anywhere on the earth's surface and ask her or him if the Algerian people have not already acquired the right to be twenty times independent. There is no one, in 1959, apart from those Frenchmen who have dragged their country into this horrible adventure, who does not yearn to see the end of this slaughter and the birth of the Algerian nation.

Nevertheless, there is no end in sight, and we know that the French Army is preparing a series of offensives for the coming months. The war goes on.

Men are therefore entitled to wonder what are the reasons for this obstinacy. One has the duty to understand this entrenchment in a war which has all the earmarks of a morbid infatuation. We want to show in this first study that on the Algerian soil a new society has come to birth. The men and women of Algeria today resemble neither those of 1930 nor those of 1954, nor yet those of 1957. The old Algeria is dead. All the innocent

[8] Previously Europeans and natives in Algeria had been elected separately, to separate "colleges" having different powers. (Translator's note)

blood that has flowed onto the national soil has produced a new humanity and no one must fail to recognize this fact.

Having once affirmed that it "would not hand over to the Arabs one million of its sons," France today proclaims that it will never abandon the Sahara and its resources. Such arguments, to be sure, carry no weight with the Algerian. He replies that the richness of a country is not an excuse for oppressing it.

We shall show that the form and the content of national existence already exist in Algeria and that there can be no turning back. While in many colonial countries it is the independence acquired by a party that progressively informs the diffused national consciousness of the people, in Algeria it is the national consciousness, the collective sufferings and terrors that make it inevitable that the people must take its destiny into its own hands.

Algeria is virtually independent. The Algerians already consider themselves sovereign.

It remains for France to recognize her. This is obviously of utmost importance. But the real situation too is important. It deserves to be known, for it fundamentally limits the military or political hopes of French colonialism.

Why does the French government not put an end to the Algerian war? Why does it refuse to negotiate with the members of the Algerian government? Such are the questions that an honest man, in 1959, is entitled to ask.

It is not enough to say that colonialism is still powerful in France. It is not sufficient to say that the Sahara has modified the facts of the problem.

All this is true, but there is something else. It seems to us that in Algeria the principal point on which men of good will and the French government stumble is the European minority. This is why we have devoted a whole chapter to this question.

Algeria is a settlers' colony. The last settlers' colony to be talked about was South Africa. The points made are familiar to all.

Algeria's Europeans have never quite given up hope of breaking with France and of imposing their iron law on the Algerians. It is the sole constant of the colonialist policy in Algeria. Today the French Army is won over to this idea. The rumors of peace that spring up here and there must therefore not be taken seriously.

France will make peace in Algeria by strengthening its domination over Algeria *or by smashing the European feudal interests in Algeria.* Apart from these two solutions, peace will have to be imposed upon it internationally through the agency of the United Nations or militarily by the Algerian forces.

We can see therefore that peace is not for tomorrow. We shall show that France cannot resume its domination in Algeria, even if this domination were to be lightened and dissimulated. The French government is doomed either to oppose a few hundred war criminals or else to give increasing support to the genocide that is rife in Algeria.

The French authorities do not make us smile when they declare that "the rebellion has a strength of twenty-five thousand men." What do all these figures amount to when balanced against the holy and colossal energy that keeps a whole people at the boiling point? Even if it is proven that our forces do not exceed five thousand poorly armed men, what value can such knowledge have since, with a million weapons, we should still be creating malcontents? Hundreds of thousands of other Algerian men and women would not forgive the leaders for not enrolling them, for leaving them unarmed. What would the Algerian government be if it did not have the people behind it?

The French authorities have recently officially recognized the existence of one million displaced, regrouped Algerians. They wanted to cut the army off from the people. They wanted, so it appears, to avoid the "rotting of Algeria." But how far can one go?

One million hostages behind barbed wires, and now the French themselves sound the alarm: "Medication no longer has any effect on these regrouped people, so great is their physiological deterioration." What then? Colonialism is fighting to strengthen its domination and human and economic exploitation. It is fighting also to maintain the identity of the image it has of the Algerian and the depreciated image that the Algerian had of himself. Well, this has long since become impossible.

The Algerian nation is no longer in a future heaven. It is no longer the product of hazy and phantasy-ridden imaginations. It is at the very center of the new Algerian man. *There is a new kind of Algerian man,* a new dimension to his existence.

The thesis that men change at the same time that they change the world has never been so manifest as it is now in Algeria. This trial of strength not only remodels the consciousness that man has of himself, and of his former dominators or of the world, at last within his reach.

This struggle at different levels renews the symbols, the myths, the beliefs, the emotional responsiveness of the people. We witness in Algeria man's reassertion of his capacity to progress.

Who can hope to arrest this essential movement? Is it not better to open one's eyes and see the magnificence, but also the naturalness, of this evolution?

Are we still living in the time when man must fight and die in order to have the right to be the citizen of a nation?

Is anything more grotesque and humiliating and obscene than the appellation, "French-Moslems"?

And the wretchedness, the indignity, kept alive and nourished every morning—is this not a sufficient pretext for the most far-fetched crimes?

Are there, then, not enough people on this earth resolved to impose reason on this unreason?

"The possibility of victory over the rebellion can no longer be ruled out," General Challe proclaims. Irony here would be out of place. All the generals-in-chief of all the colonial wars repeat the same things, but how can they fail to understand that no rebellion is ever vanquished? What can it possibly mean, to vanquish a rebellion?

They tried to vanquish the U.P.C.[4], but did not the Cameroons win their independence? The only difference is that colonialism, before it left, sowed half-treasons, prevarications, rancors in profusion among the Cameroonian people. As a result, the future of the Cameroons is jeopardized for several years to come by an evil and outwardly subtle policy.

We want to show in these pages that *colonialism has definitely lost out in Algeria, while the Algerians, come what may, have definitely won.*

This people, which was lost to history, once again finds a flag, a government already recognized by many States, and it can now no longer draw back. This illiterate people that is writing the finest and the most stirring pages of the struggle for freedom cannot draw back nor be silent.

French colonialism must know these things. It can no longer hide from itself the fact that the Algerian government can mobilize any Algerian at any time. Even the winners in the last elections, forcibly registered on the administration's electoral lists, would resign if ordered to do so by the F.L.N.[5] Not even the deputies of the 13th of May can long resist the new national authority. What then? An army can at any time reconquer the ground lost, but how can the inferiority complex, the fear and the despair of the past be reimplanted in the consciousness of the people? How can one imagine, as General de Gaulle ingenuously invited them to do, that the Algerians will "go back to their homes"? What meaning can this expression have for an Algerian of today?

Colonialism shuts its eyes to the real facts of the problem. It imagines that our power is measured by the number of our heavy machine guns. This was true in the first months of 1955.

[4] U.P.C.—Union of Cameroon Populations. A party agitating for independence. (Translator's note)

[5] F.L.N.—the National Liberation Front. (Translator's note)

It is no longer true today. First of all, because other elements have their weight in the scales of history. Next, because machine guns and cannons are no longer the weapons of the colonialist alone.

Two-thirds of the world's population is ready to give to the Revolution as many heavy machine-guns as we need. And if the other third does not do so, it is by no means because it is out of sympathy with the cause of the Algerian people. Quite to the contrary, this other third misses no opportunity to make it known that this cause has its unqualified moral support. And it finds ways of expressing this concretely.

The power of the Algerian Revolution henceforth resides in the radical mutation that the Algerian has undergone.

General de Gaulle, addressing himself to Algeria's extremists recently, declared that "Papa's Algeria is dead." That is quite true. But it is not the whole truth. Big Brother's Algeria is dead too. There is a new Algeria, an Algerian nation, an Algerian government. These obvious facts will sooner or later have to be recognized.

We shall see in these pages what transformations the consciousness of the Algerian has undergone. We shall see the fissures that, as they have grown, have been the harbingers of Algeria's new European society. What we are really witnessing is the slow but sure agony of the settler mentality.

The new relations are not the result of one barbarism replacing another barbarism, of one crushing of man replacing another crushing of man. What we Algerians want is to discover the man behind the colonizer; this man who is both the organizer and the victim of a system that has choked him and reduced him to silence. As for us, we have long since rehabilitated the Algerian colonized man. We have wrenched the Algerian man from a centuries-old and implacable oppression. We have risen to our feet and we are now moving forward. Who can settle us back in servitude?

We want an Algeria open to all, in which every kind of genius may grow.

This is what we want and this is what we shall achieve. We do not believe there exists anywhere a force capable of standing in our way.

Frantz Fanon

July 1959

1

Algeria Unveiled

The way people clothe themselves, together with the traditions of dress and finery that custom implies, constitutes the most distinctive form of a society's uniqueness, that is to say the one that is the most immediately perceptible. Within the general pattern of a given costume, there are of course always modifications of detail, innovations which in highly developed societies are the mark of fashion. But the effect as a whole remains homogeneous, and great areas of civilization, immense cultural regions, can be grouped together on the basis of original, specific techniques of men's and women's dress.

It is by their apparel that types of society first become known, whether through written accounts and photographic records or motion pictures. Thus, there are civilizations without neckties, civilizations with loin-cloths, and others without hats. The fact of belonging to a given cultural group is usually revealed by clothing traditions. In the Arab world, for example, the veil worn by women is at once noticed by the tourist. One may remain for a long time unaware of the fact that a Moslem does not eat pork or that he denies himself daily sexual relations during the month of Ramadan, but the veil worn by the women appears with such constancy that it generally suffices to characterize Arab society.

In the Arab Maghreb, the veil belongs to the clothing traditions of the Tunisian, Algerian, Moroccan and Libyan national societies. For the tourist and the foreigner, the veil demarcates both Algerian society and its feminine component.[1] In the case of the Algerian man, on the other hand, regional modifications can be noted: the *fez* in urban centers, turbans and *djellabas*[2] in the countryside. The masculine garb allows a certain margin of choice, a modicum of heterogeneity. The woman seen in her white veil unifies the perception that one has of Algerian feminine society. Obviously what we have here is a uniform which tolerates no modification, no variant.[3]

The *haïk*[4] very clearly demarcates the Algerian colonized society. It is of course possible to remain hesitant before a little girl, but all uncertainty vanishes at the time of puberty. With the veil, things become well-defined and ordered. The Algerian woman, in the eyes of the observer, is unmistakably "she who hides behind a veil."

We shall see that this veil, one of the elements of the traditional Algerian garb, was to become the bone of contention in a grandiose battle, on account of which the occupation forces

[1] We do not here consider rural areas where the woman is often unveiled. Nor do we take into account the Kabyle woman who, except in the large cities, never uses a veil. For the tourist who rarely ventures into the mountains, the Arab woman is first of all one who wears a veil. This originality of the Kabyle woman constitutes, among others, one of the themes of colonialist propaganda bringing out the opposition between Arabs and Berbers. Such studies, devoted to the analysis of psychological modifications, neglect considerations that are properly historical. We shall presently take up this other aspect of Algerian reality in action. Here we shall content ourselves with pointing out that the Kabyle women, in the course of 130 years of domination, have developed other defense mechanisms with respect to the occupier. During the war of liberation their forms of action have likewise assumed absolutely original aspects.

[2] *Djellaba*—a long, hooded cloak. (Translator's note)

[3] One phenomenon deserves to be recalled. In the course of the Moroccan people's struggle for liberation, and chiefly in the cities, the white veil was replaced by the black veil. This important modification is explained by the Moroccan women's desire to express their attachment to His Majesty Mohammed V. It will be remembered that it was immediately after the exiling of the King of Morocco that the black veil, a sign of mourning, made its appearance. It is worth noting that black, in Moroccan or Arab society, has never expressed mourning or affliction. As a combat measure, the adoption of black is a response to the desire to exert a symbolic pressure on the occupier, and hence to make a logical choice of one's own symbols.

[4] The *haïk*—the Arab name for the big square veil worn by Arab women, covering the face and the whole body. (Translator's note)

were to mobilize their most powerful and most varied resources, and in the course of which the colonized were to display a surprising force of inertia. Taken as a whole, colonial society, with its values, its areas of strength, and its philosophy, reacts to the veil in a rather homogeneous way. The decisive battle was launched before 1954, more precisely during the early 1930's. The officials of the French administration in Algeria, committed to destroying the people's originality, and under instructions to bring about the disintegration, at whatever cost, of forms of existence likely to evoke a national reality directly or indirectly, were to concentrate their efforts on the wearing of the veil, which was looked upon at this juncture as a symbol of the status of the Algerian woman. Such a position is not the consequence of a chance intuition. It is on the basis of the analyses of sociologists and ethnologists that the specialists in so-called native affairs and the heads of the Arab Bureaus coordinated their work. At an initial stage, there was a pure and simple adoption of the well-known formula, "Let's win over the women and the rest will follow." This definition of policy merely gave a scientific coloration to the "discoveries" of the sociologists.[5]

Beneath the patrilineal pattern of Algerian society, the specialists described a structure of matrilineal essence. Arab society has often been presented by Westerners as a formal society in which outside appearances are paramount. The Algerian woman, an intermediary between obscure forces and the group, appeared in this perspective to assume a primordial importance. Behind the visible, manifest patriarchy, the more significant existence of a basic matriarchy was affirmed. The role of the Algerian mother, that of the grandmother, the aunt and the "old woman," were inventoried and defined.

This enabled the colonial administration to define a precise political doctrine: "If we want to destroy the structure of Algerian society, its capacity for resistance, we must first of all con-

[5] See Appendix at the end of this chapter.

quer the women; we must go and find them behind the veil where they hide themselves and in the houses where the men keep them out of sight." It is the situation of woman that was accordingly taken as the theme of action. The dominant administration solemnly undertook to defend this woman, pictured as humiliated, sequestered, cloistered . . . It described the immense possibilities of woman, unfortunately transformed by the Algerian man into an inert, demonetized, indeed dehumanized object. The behavior of the Algerian was very firmly denounced and described as medieval and barbaric. With infinite science, a blanket indictment against the "sadistic and vampirish" Algerian attitude toward women was prepared and drawn up. Around the family life of the Algerian, the occupier piled up a whole mass of judgments, appraisals, reasons, accumulated anecdotes and edifying examples, thus attempting to confine the Algerian within a circle of guilt.

Mutual aid societies and societies to promote solidarity with Algerian women sprang up in great number. Lamentations were organized. "We want to make the Algerian ashamed of the fate that he metes out to women." This was a period of effervescence, of putting into application a whole technique of infiltration, in the course of which droves of social workers and women directing charitable works descended on the Arab quarters.

The indigent and famished women were the first to be besieged. Every kilo of semolina distributed was accompanied by a dose of indignation against the veil and the cloister. The indignation was followed up by practical advice. Algerian women were invited to play "a functional, capital role" in the transformation of their lot. They were pressed to say no to a centuries-old subjection. The immense role they were called upon to play was described to them. The colonial administration invested great sums in this combat. After it had been posited that the woman constituted the pivot of Algerian society, all efforts were made to obtain control over her. The Algerian, it was assured, would not stir, would resist the task of cultural destruction undertaken by the occupier, would oppose assimilation, so long as his woman had not reversed the stream. In the colonialist program, it was the woman who was given the historic mission of shaking up the Algerian man. Converting the woman, winning her over to the foreign values, wrenching her free from her status, was at the same time achieving a real power over the man and attaining a practical, effective means of destructuring Algerian culture.

Still today, in 1959, the dream of a total domestication of Algerian society by means of "unveiled women aiding and sheltering the occupier" continues to haunt the colonial authorities.[6]

The Algerian men, for their part, are a target of criticism for their European comrades, or more officially for their bosses. There is not a European worker who does not sooner or later, in the give and take of relations on the job site, the shop or the office, ask the Algerian the ritual questions: "Does your wife wear the veil? Why don't you take your wife to the movies, to the fights, to the café?"

European bosses do not limit themselves to the disingenuous query or the glancing invitation. They use "Indian cunning" to corner the Algerian and push him to painful decisions. In connection with a holiday—Christmas or New Year, or simply a

[6] The ground is prepared in the school establishments as well. The teachers to whom the parents have entrusted their children soon acquire the habit of passing severe judgment on the fate of woman in Algerian society. "We firmly hope that you at least will be strong enough to impose your point of view. . . . " Schools for "young Moslem girls" are multiplying. At their pupils' approach to puberty, the teachers or the nuns exercise a truly exceptional activity. The mothers are first felt out, besieged, and given the mission of shaking up and convincing the father. Much is made of the young student's prodigious intelligence, her maturity; a picture is painted of the brilliant future that awaits those eager young creatures, and it is none too subtly hinted that it would be criminal if the child's schooling were interrupted. The shortcomings of colonized society are conceded, and it is proposed that the young student be sent to boarding school in order to spare the parents the criticism of "narrow-minded neighbors." For the specialist in colonial affairs, veterans and the "developed" natives are the commandos who are entrusted with destroying the cultural resistance of a colonized country. The regions are accordingly classified in terms of the number of developed "active units," in other words, agents of erosion of the national culture that they contain.

social occasion with the firm—the boss will invite *the Algerian employe and his wife*. The invitation is not a collective one. Every Algerian is called in to the director's office and invited by name to come with "your little family." "The firm being one big family, it would be unseemly for some to come without their wives, you understand? . . ." Before this formal summons, the Algerian sometimes experiences moments of difficulty. If he comes with his wife, it means admitting defeat, it means "prostituting his wife," exhibiting her, abandoning a mode of resistance. On the other hand, going alone means refusing to give satisfaction to the boss; it means running the risk of being out of a job. The study of a case chosen at random—a description of the traps set by the European in order to bring the Algerian to expose himself, to declare: "My wife wears a veil, she shall not go out," or else to betray: "Since you want to see her, here she is,"—would bring out the sadistic and perverse character of these contacts and relationships and would show in microcosm the tragedy of the colonial situation on the psychological level, the way the two systems directly confront each other, the epic of the colonized society, with its specific ways of existing, in the face of the colonialist hydra.

With the Algerian intellectual, the aggressiveness appears in its full intensity. The *fellah,* "the passive slave of a rigidly structured group," is looked upon with a certain indulgence by the conqueror.[7] The lawyer and the doctor, on the other hand, are severely frowned upon. These intellectuals, who keep their wives in a state of semi-slavery, are literally pointed to with an accusing finger. Colonial society blazes up vehemently against this inferior status of the Algerian woman. Its members worry and show concern for those unfortunate women, doomed "to produce brats," kept behind walls, banned.

Before the Algerian intellectual, racialist arguments spring forth with special readiness. For all that he is a doctor, people will say, he still remains an Arab. "You can't get away from nature." Illustrations of this kind of race prejudice can be mul-

[7] *fellah*—a peasant. (Translator's note)

tiplied indefinitely. Clearly, the intellectual is reproached for limiting the extension of learned Western habits, for not playing his role as an active agent of upheaval of the colonized society, for not giving his wife the benefit of the privileges of a more worthy and meaningful life. . . . In the large population centers it is altogether commonplace to hear a European confess acidly that he has never seen the wife of an Algerian he has known for twenty years. At a more diffuse, but highly revealing, level of apprehension, we find the bitter observation that "we work in vain" . . . that "Islam holds its prey."

The method of presenting the Algerian as a prey fought over with equal ferocity by Islam and France with its Western culture reveals the whole approach of the occupier, his philosophy and his policy. This expression indicates that the occupier, smarting from his failures, presents in a simplified and pejorative way the system of values by means of which the colonized person resists his innumerable offensives. What is in fact the assertion of a distinct identity, concern with keeping intact a few shreds of national existence, is attributed to religious, magical, fanatical behavior.

This rejection of the conqueror assumes original forms, according to circumstances or to the type of colonial situation. On the whole, these forms of behavior have been fairly well studied in the course of the past twenty years; it cannot be said, however, that the conclusions that have been reached are wholly valid. Specialists in basic education for underdeveloped countries or technicians for the advancement of retarded societies would do well to understand the sterile and harmful character of any endeavor which illuminates preferentially a given element of the colonized society. Even within the framework of a newly independent nation, one cannot attack this or that segment of the cultural whole without endangering the work undertaken (leaving aside the question of the native's psychological balance). More precisely, the phenomena of counter-acculturation must be understood as the organic impossibility of a culture to modify any one of its customs without at the same time re-evaluating its deepest values, its most stable models. To speak of counter-acculturation in a colonial situation is an absurdity. The phenomena of resistance observed in the colonized must be related to an attitude of counter-assimilation, of maintenance of a cultural, hence national, originality.

The occupying forces, in applying their maximum psychological attention to the veil worn by Algerian women, were obviously bound to achieve some results. Here and there it thus happened that a woman was "saved," and symbolically unveiled.

These test-women, with bare faces and free bodies, henceforth circulated like sound currency in the European society of Algeria. These women were surrounded by an atmosphere of newness. The Europeans, over-excited and wholly given over to their victory, carried away in a kind of trance, would speak of the psychological phenomena of conversion. And in fact, in the European society, the agents of this conversion were held in esteem. They were envied. The benevolent attention of the administration was drawn to them.

After each success, the authorities were strengthened in their conviction that the Algerian woman would support Western penetration into the native society. Every rejected veil disclosed to the eyes of the colonialists horizons until then forbidden, and revealed to them, piece by piece, the flesh of Algeria laid bare. The occupier's aggressiveness, and hence his hopes, multiplied ten-fold each time a new face was uncovered. Every new Algerian woman unveiled announced to the occupier an Algerian society whose systems of defense were in the process of dislocation, open and breached. Every veil that fell, every body that became liberated from the traditional embrace of the *haïk,* every face that offered itself to the bold and impatient glance of the occupier, was a negative expression of the fact that Algeria was beginning to deny herself and was accepting the rape of the colonizer. Algerian society with every abandoned veil seemed to express its willingness to attend the master's school and to decide to change its habits under the occupier's direction and patronage.

We have seen how colonial society, the colonial administration, perceives the veil, and we have sketched the dynamics of the efforts undertaken to fight it as an institution and the resistances developed by the colonized society. At the level of the individual, of the private European, it may be interesting to follow the multiple reactions provoked by the existence of the veil, which reveal the original way in which the Algerian woman manages to be present or absent.

For a European not directly involved in this work of conversion, what reactions are there to be recorded?

The dominant attitude appears to us to be a romantic exoticism, strongly tinged with sensuality.

And, to begin with, the veil hides a beauty.

A revealing reflection—among others—of this state of mind was communicated to us by a European visiting Algeria who, in the exercise of his profession (he was a lawyer), had had the opportunity of seeing a few Algerian women without the veil. These men, he said, speaking of the Algerians, are guilty of concealing so many strange beauties. It was his conclusion that a people with a cache of such prizes, of such perfections of nature, owes it to itself to show them, to exhibit them. If worst came to worst, he added, it ought to be possible to force them to do so.

A strand of hair, a bit of forehead, a segment of an "overwhelmingly beautiful" face glimpsed in a streetcar or on a train, may suffice to keep alive and strengthen the European's persistence in his irrational conviction that the Algerian woman is the queen of all women.

But there is also in the European the crystallization of an aggressiveness, the strain of a kind of violence before the Algerian woman. Unveiling this woman is revealing her beauty; it is baring her secret, breaking her resistance, making her available for adventure. Hiding the face is also disguising a secret; it is also creating a world of mystery, of the hidden. In a confused way, the European experiences his relation with the Algerian woman at a highly complex level. There is in it the will to bring this woman within his reach, to make her a possible object of possession.

This woman who sees without being seen frustrates the colonizer. There is no reciprocity. She does not yield herself, does not give herself, does not offer herself. The Algerian has an attitude toward the Algerian woman which is on the whole clear. He does not see her. There is even a permanent intention not to perceive the feminine profile, not to pay attention to women. In the case of the Algerian, therefore, there is not, in the street or on a road, that behavior characterizing a sexual encounter that is described in terms of the glance, of the physical bearing, the muscular tension, the signs of disturbance to which the phenomenology of encounters has accustomed us.

The European faced with an Algerian woman wants to see. He reacts in an aggressive way before this limitation of his perception. Frustration and aggressiveness, here too, evolve apace. Aggressiveness comes to light, in the first place, in structurally ambivalent attitudes and in the dream material that can be revealed in the European, whether he is normal or suffers from neuropathological disturbances.[8]

In a medical consultation, for example, at the end of the

[8] Attention must be called to a frequent attitude, on the part of European women in particular, with regard to a special category of evolved natives. Certain unveiled Algerian women turn themselves into perfect Westerners with amazing rapidity and unsuspected ease. European women feel a certain uneasiness in the presence of these women. Frustrated in the presence of the veil, they experience a similar impression before the bared face, before that unabashed body which has lost all awkwardness, all timidity, and become downright offensive. Not only is the satisfaction of supervising the evolution and correcting the mistakes of the unveiled woman withdrawn from the European woman, but she feels herself challenged on the level of feminine charm, of elegance, and even sees a competitor in this novice metamorphosed into a professional, a neophyte transformed into a propagandist. The European woman has no choice but to make common cause with the Algerian man who had fiercely flung the unveiled woman into the camp of evil and of depravation. "Really!" the European women will exclaim, "these unveiled women are quite amoral and shameless." Integration, in order to be successful, seems indeed to have to be simply a continued, accepted paternalism.

morning, it is common to hear European doctors express their disappointment. The women who remove their veils before them are commonplace, vulgar; there is really nothing to make such a mystery of. One wonders what they are hiding.

European women settle the conflict in a much less roundabout way. They bluntly affirm that no one hides what is beautiful and discern in this strange custom an "altogether feminine" intention of disguising imperfections. And they proceed to compare the strategy of the European woman, which is intended to correct, to embellish, to bring out (beauty treatments, hairdos, fashion), with that of the Algerian woman, who prefers to veil, to conceal, to cultivate the man's doubt and desire. On another level, it is claimed that the intention is to mislead the customer, and that the wrapping in which the "merchandise" is presented does not really alter its nature, nor its value.

The content of the dreams of Europeans brings out other special themes. Jean-Paul Sartre, in his *Réflections Sur la Question Juive,* has shown that on the level of the unconscious, the Jewish woman almost always has an aura of rape about her.

The history of the French conquest in Algeria, including the overrunning of villages by the troops, the confiscation of property and the raping of women, the pillaging of a country, has contributed to the birth and the crystallization of the same dynamic image. At the level of the psychological strata of the occupier, the evocation of this freedom given to the sadism of the conqueror, to his eroticism, creates faults, fertile gaps through which both dreamlike forms of behavior and, on certain occasions, criminal acts can emerge.

Thus the rape of the Algerian woman in the dream of a European is always preceded by a rending of the veil. We here witness a double deflowering. Likewise, the woman's conduct is never one of consent or acceptance, but of abject humility.

Whenever, in dreams having an erotic content, a European meets an Algerian woman, the specific features of his relations with the colonized society manifest themselves. These dreams evolve neither on the same erotic plane, nor at the same tempo, as those that involve a European woman.

With an Algerian woman, there is no progressive conquest, no mutual revelation. Straight off, with the maximum of violence, there is possession, rape, near-murder. The act assumes a para-neurotic brutality and sadism, even in a normal European. This brutality and this sadism are in fact emphasized by the frightened attitude of the Algerian woman. In the dream, the woman-victim screams, struggles like a doe, and as she weakens and faints, is penetrated, martyrized, ripped apart.

Attention must likewise be drawn to a characteristic of this dream content that appears important to us. The European never dreams of an Algerian woman taken in isolation. On the rare occasions when the encounter has become a binding relationship that can be regarded as a couple, it has quickly been transformed by the desperate flight of the woman who, inevitably, leads the male "among women." The European always dreams of a group of women, of a field of women, suggestive of the gynaeceum, the harem—exotic themes deeply rooted in the unconscious.

The European's aggressiveness will express itself likewise in contemplation of the Algerian woman's morality. Her timidity and her reserve are transformed in accordance with the commonplace laws of conflictual psychology into their opposite, and the Algerian woman becomes hypocritical, perverse, and even a veritable nymphomaniac.

We have seen that on the level of individuals the colonial strategy of destructuring Algerian society very quickly came to assign a prominent place to the Algerian woman. The colonialist's relentlessness, his methods of struggle were bound to give rise to reactionary forms of behavior on the part of the colonized. In the face of the violence of the occupier, the colonized found himself defining a principled position with respect to a formerly inert element of the native cultural configuration. It was the colonialist's frenzy to unveil the Algerian woman, it was his gamble on winning the battle of the veil at whatever cost, that were to provoke the native's bristling resistance. The deliberately aggressive intentions of the colonialist with respect to the *haïk* gave a new life to this dead element of the Algerian cultural stock—dead because stabilized, without any progressive change in form or color. We here recognize one of the laws of the psychology of colonization. In an initial phase, it is the action, the plans of the occupier that determine the centers of resistance around which a people's will to survive becomes organized.

It is the white man who creates the Negro. But it is the Negro who creates negritude. To the colonialist offensive against the veil, the colonized opposes the cult of the veil. What was an undifferentiated element in a homogeneous whole acquires a taboo character, and the attitude of a given Algerian woman with respect to the veil will be constantly related to her overall attitude with respect to the foreign occupation. The colonized, in the face of the emphasis given by the colonialist to this or that aspect of his traditions, reacts very violently. The attention devoted to modifying this aspect, the emotion the conqueror puts into his pedagogical work, his prayers, his threats, weave a whole universe of resistances around this particular element of the culture. Holding out against the occupier on this precise element means inflicting upon him a spectacular setback; it means more particularly maintaining "co-existence" as a form of conflict and latent warfare. It means keeping up the atmosphere of an armed truce.

Upon the outbreak of the struggle for liberation, the attitude of the Algerian woman, or of native society in general, with regard to the veil was to undergo important modifications. These innovations are of particular interest in view of the fact that they were at no time included in the program of the struggle. The doctrine of the Revolution, the strategy of combat, never postulated the necessity for a revision of forms of behavior with respect to the veil. We are able to affirm even now that when Algeria has gained her independence such questions will not be raised, for in the practice of the Revolution the people have understood that problems are resolved in the very movement that raises them.

Until 1955, the combat was waged exclusively by the men. The revolutionary characteristics of this combat, the necessity for absolute secrecy, obliged the militant to keep his woman in absolute ignorance. As the enemy gradually adapted himself to the forms of combat, new difficulties appeared which required original solutions. The decision to involve women as active elements of the Algerian Revolution was not reached lightly. In a sense, it was the very conception of the combat that had to be modified. The violence of the occupier, his ferocity, his delirious attachment to the national territory, induced the leaders no longer to exclude certain forms of combat. Progressively, the urgency of a total war made itself felt. But involving the women was not solely a response to the desire to mobilize the entire nation. The women's entry into the war had to be harmonized with respect for the revolutionary nature of the war. In other words, the women had to show as much spirit of sacrifice as the men. It was therefore necessary to have the same confidence in them as was required from seasoned militants who had served several prison sentences. A moral elevation and a strength of character that were altogether exceptional would therefore be required of the women. There was no lack of hesitations. The revolutionary wheels had assumed such proportions; the mechanism was running at a given rate. The machine would have to be complicated; in other words its network would have to be extended without affecting its efficiency. The women could not be conceived of as a replacement product, but as an element capable of adequately meeting the new tasks.

In the mountains, women helped the *guerrilla* during halts or when convalescing after a wound or a case of typhoid contracted in the *djebel*.[9] But deciding to incorporate women as essential elements, to have the Revolution depend on their presence and their action in this or that sector, was obviously a

[9] *djebel*—mountain. (Translator's note)

wholly revolutionary step. To have the Revolution rest at any point on their activity was an important choice.

Such a decision was made difficult for several reasons. During the whole period of unchallenged domination, we have seen that Algerian society, and particularly the women, had a tendency to flee from the occupier. The tenacity of the occupier in his endeavor to unveil the women, to make of them an ally in the work of cultural destruction, had the effect of strengthening the traditional patterns of behavior. These patterns, which were essentially positive in the strategy of resistance to the corrosive action of the colonizer, naturally had negative effects. The woman, especially the city woman, suffered a loss of ease and of assurance. Having been accustomed to confinement, her body did not have the normal mobility before a limitless horizon of avenues, of unfolded sidewalks, of houses, of people dodged or bumped into. This relatively cloistered life, with its known, categorized, regulated comings and goings, made any immediate revolution seem a dubious proposition. The political leaders were perfectly familiar with these problems, and their hesitations expressed their consciousness of their responsibilities. They were entitled to doubt the success of this measure. Would not such a decision have catastrophic consequences for the progress of the Revolution?

To this doubt there was added an equally important element. The leaders hesitated to involve the women, being perfectly aware of the ferocity of the colonizer. The leaders of the Revolution had no illusions as to the enemy's criminal capacities. Nearly all of them had passed through their jails or had had sessions with survivors from the camps or the cells of the French judicial police. No one of them failed to realize that any Algerian woman arrested would be tortured to death. It is relatively easy to commit oneself to this path and to accept among different eventualities that of dying under torture. The matter is a little more difficult when it involves designating someone who manifestly runs the risk of certain death. But the decision as to whether or not the women were to participate in the Revolution had to be made; the inner oppositions became massive, and each decision gave rise to the same hesitations, produced the same despair.

In the face of the extraordinary success of this new form of popular combat, observers have compared the action of the Algerian women to that of certain women resistance fighters or even secret agents of the specialized services. It must be constantly borne in mind that the committed Algerian woman learns both her role as "a woman alone in the street" and her revolutionary mission instinctively. The Algerian woman is not a secret agent. It is without apprenticeship, without briefing, without fuss, that she goes out into the street with three grenades in her handbag or the activity report of an area in her bodice. She does not have the sensation of playing a role she has read about ever so many times in novels, or seen in motion pictures. There is not that coefficient of play, of imitation, almost always present in this form of action when we are dealing with a Western woman.

What we have here is not the bringing to light of a character known and frequented a thousand times in imagination or in stories. It is an authentic birth in a pure state, without preliminary instruction. There is no character to imitate. On the contrary, there is an intense dramatization, a continuity between the woman and the revolutionary. The Algerian woman rises directly to the level of tragedy.[10]

The growth in number of the F.L.N. cells, the range of new tasks—finance, intelligence, counter-intelligence, political training—the necessity to provide for one active cell three or four replacement cells to be held in reserve, ready to become active at the slightest alert concerning the front cell, obliged the leaders to seek other avenues for the carrying out of strictly individ-

[10] We are mentioning here only realities known to the enemy. We therefore say nothing about the new forms of action adopted by women in the Revolution. Since 1958, in fact, the tortures inflicted on women militants have enabled the occupier to have an idea of the strategy used by women. Today new adaptations have developed. It will therefore be understood if we are silent as to these.

ual assignments. After a final series of meetings among leaders, and especially in view of the urgency of the daily problems that the Revolution faced, the decision to concretely involve women in the national struggle was reached.

The revolutionary character of this decision must once again be emphasized. At the beginning, it was the married women who were contacted. But rather soon these restrictions were abandoned. The married women whose husbands were militants were the first to be chosen. Later, widows or divorced women were designated. In any case, there were never any unmarried girls—first of all, because a girl of even twenty or twenty-three hardly ever has occasion to leave the family domicile unaccompanied. But the woman's duties as mother or spouse, the desire to limit to the minimum the possible consequences of her arrest and her death, and also the more and more numerous volunteering of unmarried girls, led the political leaders to make another leap, to remove all restrictions, to accept indiscriminately the support of all Algerian women.

Meanwhile the woman who might be acting as a liaison agent, as a bearer of tracts, as she walked some hundred or two hundred meters ahead of the man under whose orders she was working, still wore a veil; but after a certain period the pattern of activity that the struggle involved shifted in the direction of the European city. The protective mantle of the Kasbah, the almost organic curtain of safety that the Arab town weaves round the native, withdrew, and the Algerian woman, exposed, was sent forth into the conqueror's city. Very quickly she adopted an absolutely unbelievable offensive tactic. When colonized people undertake an action against the oppressor, and when this oppression is exercised in the form of exacerbated and continuous violence as in Algeria, they must overcome a considerable number of taboos. The European city is not the prolongation of the native city. The colonizers have not settled in the midst of the natives. They have surrounded the native city; they have laid siege to it. Every exit from the

Kasbah of Algiers opens on enemy territory. And so it is in Constantine, in Oran, in Blida, in Bone.

The native cities are deliberately caught in the conqueror's vise. To get an idea of the rigor with which the immobilizing of the native city, of the autochthonous population, is organized, one must have in one's hands the plans according to which a colonial city has been laid out, and compare them with the comments of the general staff of the occupation forces.

Apart from the charwomen employed in the conquerors' homes, those whom the colonizer indiscriminately calls the "Fatmas," the Algerian women, especially the young Algerian women, rarely venture into the European city. Their movements are almost entirely limited to the Arab city. And even in the Arab city their movements are reduced to the minimum. The rare occasions on which the Algerian woman abandons the city are almost always in connection with some event, either of an exceptional nature (the death of a relative residing in a nearby locality), or, more often, traditional family visits for religious feasts, or a pilgrimage. In such cases, the European city is crossed in a car, usually early in the morning. The Algerian woman, the young Algerian woman—except for a very few students (who, besides, never have the same ease as their European counterparts)—must overcome a multiplicity of inner resistances, of subjectively organized fears, of emotions. She must at the same time confront the essentially hostile world of the occupier and the mobilized, vigilant, and efficient police forces. Each time she ventures into the European city, the Algerian woman must achieve a victory over herself, over her childish fears. She must consider the image of the occupier lodged somewhere in her mind and in her body, remodel it, initiate the essential work of eroding it, make it inessential, remove something of the shame that is attached to it, devalidate it.

Initially subjective, the breaches made in colonialism are the result of a victory of the colonized over their old fear and over the atmosphere of despair distilled day after day by a colonialism that has incrusted itself with the *prospect of enduring forever.*

The young Algerian woman, whenever she is called upon, establishes a link. Algiers is no longer the Arab city, but the autonomous area of Algiers, the nervous system of the enemy apparatus. Oran, Constantine develop their dimensions. In launching the struggle, the Algerian is loosening the vise that was tightening around the native cities. From one area of Algiers to another, from the Ruisseau to Hussein-Dey, from El-Biar to the rue Michelet, the Revolution creates new links. More and more, it is the Algerian woman, the Algerian girl, who will be assuming these tasks.

Among the tasks entrusted to the Algerian woman is the bearing of messages, of complicated verbal orders learned by heart, sometimes despite complete absence of schooling. But she is also called upon to stand watch, for an hour and often more, before a house where district leaders are conferring.

During those interminable minutes when she must avoid standing still, so as not to attract attention, and avoid venturing too far since she is responsible for the safety of the brothers within, incidents that are at once funny and pathetic are not infrequent. An unveiled Algerian girl who "walks the street" is very often noticed by young men who behave like young men all over the world, but who use a special approach as the result of the idea people habitually have of one who has discarded the veil. She is treated to unpleasant, obscene, humiliating remarks. When such things happen, she must grit her teeth, walk away a few steps, elude the passers-by who draw attention to her, who give other passers-by the desire either to follow their example, or to come to her defense. Or it may be that the Algerian woman is carrying in her bag or in a small suitcase twenty, thirty, forty million francs, money belonging to the Revolution, money which is to be used to take care of the needs of the families of prisoners, or to buy medicine and supplies for the guerrillas.

This revolutionary activity has been carried on by the Algerian woman with exemplary constancy, self-mastery, and success. Despite the inherent, subjective difficulties and notwithstanding the sometimes violent incomprehension of a part of the family, the Algerian woman assumes all the tasks entrusted to her.

But things were gradually to become more complicated. Thus the unit leaders who go into the town and who avail themselves of the women-scouts, of the girls whose function it is to lead the way, are no longer new to political activity, are no longer unknown to the police. Authentic military chiefs have now begun to pass through the cities. These are known, and are being looked for. There is not a police superintendent who does not have their pictures on his desk.

These soldiers on the move, these fighters, always carry their weapons—automatic pistols, revolvers, grenades, sometimes all three. The political leader must overcome much resistance in order to induce these men, who under no circumstance would allow themselves to be taken prisoner, to entrust their weapons to the girl who is to walk ahead of them, it being up to them, if things go badly, to recover the arms immediately. The group accordingly makes its way into the European city. A hundred meters ahead, a girl may be carrying a suitcase and behind her are two or three ordinary-looking men. This girl who is the group's lighthouse and barometer gives warning in case of danger. The file makes its way by fits and starts; police cars and patrols cruise back and forth.

There are times, as these soldiers have admitted after completing such a mission, when the urge to recover their weapons is almost irresistible because of the fear of being caught short and not having time to defend themselves. With this phase, the Algerian woman penetrates a little further into the flesh of the Revolution.

But it was from 1956 on that her activity assumed really gigantic dimensions. Having to react in rapid succession to the massacre of Algerian civilians in the mountains and in the cities, the revolutionary leadership found that if it wanted to prevent the people from being gripped by terror it had no choice but to adopt forms of terror which until then it had rejected. This phenomenon has not been sufficiently analyzed; not enough attention has been given to the reasons that lead a revolutionary movement to choose the weapon that is called terrorism.

During the French Resistance, terrorism was aimed at soldiers, at Germans of the Occupation, or at strategic enemy installations. The technique of terrorism is the same. It consists of individual or collective attempts by means of bombs or by the derailing of trains. In Algeria, where European settlers are numerous and where the territorial militias lost no time in enrolling the postman, the nurse and the grocer in the repressive system, the men who directed the struggle faced an absolutely new situation.

The decision to kill a civilian in the street is not an easy one, and no one comes to it lightly. No one takes the step of placing a bomb in a public place without a battle of conscience.

The Algerian leaders who, in view of the intensity of the repression and the frenzied character of the oppression, thought they could answer the blows received without any serious problems of conscience, discovered that the most horrible crimes do not constitute a sufficient excuse for certain decisions.

The leaders in a number of cases canceled plans or even in the last moment called off the *fidaï*[11] assigned to place a given bomb. To explain these hesitations there was, to be sure, the memory of civilians killed or frightfully wounded. There was the political consideration not to do certain things that could compromise the cause of freedom. There was also the fear that the Europeans working with the Front might be hit in these attempts. There was thus a threefold concern: not to pile up possibly innocent victims, not to give a false picture of the Revolution, and finally the anxiety to have the French democrats on their side, as well as the democrats of all the countries of the

[11] *fidaï*—a death volunteer, in the Islamic tradition. (Translator's note)

world and the Europeans of Algeria who were attracted by the Algerian national ideal.

Now the massacres of Algerians, the raids in the countryside, strengthened the assurance of the European civilians, seemed to consolidate the colonial status, and injected hope into the colonialists. The Europeans who, as a result of certain military actions on the part of the Algerian National Army in favor of the struggle of the Algerian people, had soft-pedaled their race prejudice and their insolence, recovered their old arrogance, their traditional contempt.

I remember a woman clerk in Birtouta who, on the day of the interception of the plane transporting the five members of the National Liberation Front, waved their photographs in front of her shop, shrieking: "They've been caught! They're going to get their what-you-call'ems cut off!"

Every blow dealt the Revolution, every massacre perpetrated by the adversary, intensified the ferocity of the colonialists and hemmed in the Algerian civilian on all sides.

Trains loaded with French soldiers, the French Navy on maneuvers and bombarding Algiers and Philippeville, the jet planes, the militiamen who descended on the *douars*[12] and decimated uncounted Algerians, all this contributed to giving the people the impression that they were not defended, that they were not protected, that nothing had changed, and that the Europeans could do what they wanted. This was the period when one heard Europeans announcing in the streets: "Let's each one of us take ten of them and bump them off and you'll see the problem solved in no time." And the Algerian people, especially in the cities, witnessed this boastfulness which added insult to injury and noted the impunity of these criminals who did not even take the trouble to hide. Any Algerian man or woman in a given city could in fact name the torturers and murderers of the region.

A time came when some of the people allowed doubt to enter their minds, and they began to wonder whether it was really

[12] *douar*—a village. (Translator's note)

possible, quantitatively and qualitatively, to resist the occupant's offensives. Was freedom worth the consequences of penetrating into that enormous circuit of terrorism and counter-terrorism? Did this disproportion not express the impossibility of escaping oppression?

Another part of the people, however, grew impatient and conceived the idea of putting an end to the advantage the enemy derived by pursuing the path of terror. The decision to strike the adversary individually and by name could no longer be eluded. All the prisoners "shot and killed while trying to escape," and the cries of the tortured, demanded that new forms of combat be adopted.

Members of the police and the meeting places of the colonialists (cafés in Algiers, Oran, Constantine) were the first to be singled out. From this point on the Algerian woman became wholly and deliberately immersed in the revolutionary action. It was she who would carry in her bag the grenades and the revolvers that a *fidaï* would take from her at the last moment, before the bar, or as a designated criminal passed. During this period Algerians caught in the European city were pitilessly challenged, arrested, searched.

This is why we must watch the parallel progress of this man and this woman, of this couple that brings death to the enemy, life to the Revolution. The one supporting the other, but apparently strangers to each other. The one radically transformed into a European woman, poised and unconstrained, whom no one would suspect, completely at home in the environment, and the other, a stranger, tense, moving toward his destiny.

The Algerian *fidaï,* unlike the unbalanced anarchists made famous in literature, does not take dope. The *fidaï* does not need to be unaware of danger, to befog his consciousness, or to forget. The "terrorist," from the moment he undertakes an assignment, allows death to enter into his soul. He has a rendezvous with death. The *fidaï,* on the other hand, has a rendezvous with the life of the Revolution, and with his own life. The *fidaï* is not one of the sacrificed. To be sure, he does not shrink before the possibility of losing his life or the independence of his country, but at no moment does he choose death.

If it has been decided to kill a given police superintendent responsible for tortures or a given colonialist leader, it is because these men constitute an obstacle to the progress of the Revolution. Froger, for example, symbolized a colonialist tradition and a method inaugurated at Sétif and at Guelma in 1954.[13] Moreover, Froger's apparent power crystallized the colonization and gave new life to the hopes of those who were beginning to have doubts as to the real solidity of the system. It was around people like Froger that the robbers and murderers of the Algerian people would meet and encourage one another. This was something the *fidaï* knew, and that the woman who accompanied him, his woman-arsenal, likewise knew.

Carrying revolvers, grenades, hundreds of false identity cards or bombs, the unveiled Algerian woman moves like a fish in the Western waters. The soldiers, the French patrols, smile to her as she passes, compliments on her looks are heard here and there, but no one suspects that her suitcases contain the automatic pistol which will presently mow down four or five members of one of the patrols.

We must come back to that young girl, unveiled only yesterday, who walks with sure steps down the streets of the European city teeming with policemen, parachutists, militiamen. She no longer slinks along the walls as she tended to do before the Revolution. Constantly called upon to efface herself before a member of the dominant society, the Algerian woman avoided the middle of the sidewalk which in all countries in the world belongs rightfully to those who command.

The shoulders of the unveiled Algerian woman are thrust back with easy freedom. She walks with a graceful, measured stride, neither too fast nor too slow. Her legs are bare, not confined by the veil, given back to themselves, and her hips are free.

The body of the young Algerian woman, in traditional so-

[13] Froger, one of the colonialist leaders. Executed by a *fidaï* in late 1956.

ciety, is revealed to her by its coming to maturity and by the veil. The veil covers the body and disciplines it, tempers it, at the very time when it experiences its phase of greatest effervescence. The veil protects, reassures, isolates. One must have heard the confessions of Algerian women or have analyzed the dream content of certain recently unveiled women to appreciate the importance of the veil for the body of the woman. Without the veil she has an impression of her body being cut up into bits, put adrift; the limbs seem to lengthen indefinitely. When the Algerian woman has to cross a street, for a long time she commits errors of judgment as to the exact distance to be negotiated. The unveiled body seems to escape, to dissolve. She has an impression of being improperly dressed, even of being naked. She experiences a sense of incompleteness with great intensity. She has the anxious feeling that something is unfinished, and along with this a frightful sensation of disintegrating. The absence of the veil distorts the Algerian woman's corporal pattern. She quickly has to invent new dimensions for her body, new means of muscular control. She has to create for herself an attitude of unveiled-woman-outside. She must overcome all timidity, all awkwardness (for she must pass for a European), and at the same time be careful not to overdo it, not to attract notice to herself. The Algerian woman who walks stark naked into the European city relearns her body, re-establishes it in a totally revolutionary fashion. This new dialectic of the body and of the world is primary in the case of one revolutionary woman.[14]

[14] The woman, who before the Revolution never left the house without being accompanied by her mother or her husband, is now entrusted with special missions such as going from Oran to Constantine or Algiers. For several days, all by herself, carrying directives of capital importance for the Revolution, she takes the train, spends the night with an unknown family, among militants. Here too she must harmonize her movements, for the enemy is on the lookout for any false step. But the important thing here is that the husband makes no difficulty about letting his wife leave on an assignment. He will make it, in fact, a point of pride to say to the liaison agent when the latter returns, "You see, everything has gone well in your absence." The Algerian's age-old jealousy, his "congenital" suspiciousness, have melted on contact with the Revolution. It must be pointed out also

But the Algerian woman is not only in conflict with her body. She is a link, sometimes an essential one, in the revolutionary machine. She carries weapons, knows important points of refuge. And it is in terms of the concrete dangers that she faces that we must gauge the insurmountable victories that she has had to win in order to be able to say to her chief, on her return: "Mission accomplished . . . R.A.S."[15]

Another difficulty to which attention deserves to be called appeared during the first months of feminine activity. In the course of her comings and goings, it would happen that the unveiled Algerian woman was seen by a relative or a friend of the family. The father was sooner or later informed. He would naturally hesitate to believe such allegations. Then more reports would reach him. Different persons would claim to have seen "Zohra or Fatima unveiled, walking like a . . . My Lord, protect us! . . . " The father would then decide to demand explanations. He would hardly have begun to speak when he would stop. From the young girl's look of firmness the father would have understood that her commitment was of long standing. The old fear of dishonor was swept away by a new fear, fresh and cold—that of death in battle or of torture of the girl. Behind the girl, the whole family—even the Algerian father, the authority for all things, the founder of every value—following in her footsteps, becomes committed to the new Algeria.

---

that militants who are being sought by the police take refuge with other militants not yet identified by the occupier. In such cases the woman, left alone all day with the fugitive, is the one who gets him his food, the newspapers, the mail, showing no trace of suspicion or fear. Involved in the struggle, the husband or the father learns to look upon the relations between the sexes in a new light. The militant man discovers the militant woman, and jointly they create new dimensions for Algerian society.

[15] R.A.S.—*Rien à signaler*—a military abbreviation for "Nothing to report."

We here go on to a description of attitudes. There is, however, an important piece of work to be done on the woman's role in the Revolution: the woman in the city, in the *djebel,* in the enemy administrations; the prostitute and the information she obtains; the woman in prison, under torture, facing death, before the courts. All these chapter headings, after the material has been sifted, will reveal an incalculable number of facts essential for the history of the national struggle.

Removed and reassumed again and again, the veil has been manipulated, transformed into a technique of camouflage, into a means of struggle. The virtually taboo character assumed by the veil in the colonial situation disappeared almost entirely in the course of the liberating struggle. Even Algerian women not actively integrated into the struggle formed the habit of abandoning the veil. It is true that under certain conditions, especially from 1957 on, the veil reappeared. The missions in fact became increasingly difficult. The adversary now knew, since certain militant women had spoken under torture, that a number of women very Europeanized in appearance were playing a fundamental role in the battle. Moreover, certain European women of Algeria were arrested, to the consternation of the adversary who discovered that his own system was breaking down. The discovery by the French authorities of the participation of Europeans in the liberation struggle marks a turning point in the Algerian Revolution.[16] From that day, the French patrols challenged every person. Europeans and Algerians were equally suspect. All historic limits crumbled and disappeared. Any person carrying a package could be required to open it and show its contents. Anyone was entitled to question anyone as to the nature of a parcel carried in Algiers, Philippeville, or Batna. Under those conditions it became urgent to conceal the package from the eyes of the occupier and again to cover oneself with the protective *haïk*.

Here again, a new technique had to be learned: how to carry a rather heavy object dangerous to handle under the veil and still give the impression of having one's hands free, that there was nothing under this *haïk*, except a poor woman or an insignificant young girl. It was not enough to be veiled. One had to look so much like a "fatma" that the soldier would be convinced that this woman was quite harmless.

Very difficult. Three meters ahead of you the police challenge a veiled woman who does not look particularly suspect. From the anguished expression of the unit leader you have guessed

[16] See Chapter 5.

that she is carrying a bomb, or a sack of grenades, bound to her body by a whole system of strings and straps. For the hands must be free, exhibited bare, humbly and abjectly presented to the soldiers so that they will look no further. Showing empty and apparently mobile and free hands is the sign that disarms the enemy soldier.

The Algerian woman's body, which in an initial phase was pared down, now swelled. Whereas in the previous period the body had to be made slim and disciplined to make it attractive and seductive, it now had to be squashed, made shapeless and even ridiculous. This, as we have seen, is the phase during which she undertook to carry bombs, grenades, machine-gun clips.

The enemy, however, was alerted, and in the streets one witnessed what became a commonplace spectacle of Algerian women glued to the wall, on whose bodies the famous magnetic detectors, the "frying pans," would be passed. Every veiled woman, every Algerian woman became suspect. There was no discrimination. This was the period during which men, women, children, the whole Algerian people, experienced at one and the same time their national vocation and the recasting of the new Algerian society.

Ignorant or feigning to be ignorant of these new forms of conduct, French colonialism, on the occasion of May 13th, re-enacted its old campaign of Westernizing the Algerian woman. Servants under the threat of being fired, poor women dragged from their homes, prostitutes, were brought to the public square and *symbolically* unveiled to the cries of *"Vive l'Algérie française!"* Before this new offensive old reactions reappeared. Spontaneously and without being told, the Algerian women who had long since dropped the veil once again donned the *haïk,* thus affirming that it was not true that woman liberated herself at the invitation of France and of General de Gaulle.

Behind these psychological reactions, beneath this immediate and almost unanimous response, we again see the overall attitude of rejection of the values of the occupier, even if these values objectively be worth choosing. It is because they fail to grasp this intellectual reality, this characteristic feature (the famous sensitivity of the colonized), that the colonizers rage at always "doing them good in spite of themselves." Colonialism wants everything to come from it. But the dominant psychological feature of the colonized is to withdraw before any invitation of the conqueror's. In organizing the famous cavalcade of May 13th, colonialism has obliged Algerian society to go back to methods of struggle already outmoded. In a certain sense, the different ceremonies have caused a turning back, a regression.

Colonialism must accept the fact that things happen without its control, without its direction. We are reminded of the words spoken in an international assembly by an African political figure. Responding to the standard excuse of the immaturity of colonial peoples and their incapacity to administer themselves, this man demanded for the underdeveloped peoples "the right to govern themselves badly." The doctrinal assertions of colonialism in its attempt to justify the maintenance of its domination almost always push the colonized to the position of making uncompromising, rigid, static counter-proposals.

After the 13th of May, the veil was resumed, but stripped once and for all of its exclusively traditional dimension.

There is thus a historic dynamism of the veil that is very concretely perceptible in the development of colonization in Algeria. In the beginning, the veil was a mechanism of resistance, but its value for the social group remained very strong. The veil was worn because tradition demanded a rigid separation of the sexes, but also because the occupier *was bent on unveiling Algeria.* In a second phase, the mutation occurred in connection with the Revolution and under special circumstances. The veil was abandoned in the course of revolutionary action. What had been used to block the psychological or political offensives of the occupier became a means, an instrument. The veil helped the Algerian woman to meet the new problems created by the struggle.

The colonialists are incapable of grasping the motivations of the colonized. It is the necessities of combat that give rise in Algerian society to new attitudes, to new modes of action, to new ways.

Appendix[17]

On the Algerian earth which is freeing itself day by day from the colonialist's grip, we witness a dislocation of the old myths.

Among things that are "incomprehensible" to the colonial world the case of the Algerian woman has been all too frequently mentioned. The studies of sociologists, Islam specialists and jurists are full of observations on the Algerian woman.

Described by turns as the man's slave or as the unchallenged sovereign of the home, Algerian woman and her status absorb the attention of theoreticians.

Others, of equal authority, affirm that the Algerian woman "dreams of being free," but that a retrograde and ferocious patriarchy opposes this legitimate aspiration. The most recent debates in the French National Assembly indicate the interest attached to a coherent approach to this "problem." The majority of the speakers describe the fate of the Algerian woman and demand an improvement in her status. This, it is added, is the only means of disarming the rebellion. Colonialist intellectuals consistently use the "sociological case study" approach to the colonial system. Such and such a country, they will say, called for, was crying for conquest. Thus, to take a famous example, the Madagascan was described as having a dependency complex.

As for the Algerian woman, she is "inaccessible, ambivalent, with a masochistic component." Specific behaviors are described which illustrate these different characteristics. The truth is that the study of an occupied people, militarily subject to an implacable domination, requires documentation and checking difficult

[17] This text which appeared in *Résistance Algérienne* in its issue of May 16, 1957, indicates the consciousness that the leaders of the National Liberation Front have always had of the important part played by the Algerian woman in the Revolution.

to combine. It is not the soil that is occupied. It is not the ports or the airdromes. French colonialism has settled itself in the very center of the Algerian individual and has undertaken a sustained work of cleanup, of expulsion of self, of rationally pursued mutilation.

There is not occupation of territory, on the one hand, and independence of persons on the other. It is the country as a whole, its history, its daily pulsation that are contested, disfigured, in the hope of a final destruction. Under these conditions, the individual's breathing is an observed, an occupied breathing. It is a combat breathing.

From this point on, the real values of the occupied quickly tend to acquire a clandestine form of existence. In the presence of the occupier, the occupied learns to dissemble, to resort to trickery. To the scandal of military occupation, he opposes a scandal of contact. Every contact between the occupied and the occupier is a falsehood.

In forty-eight hours the Algerian woman has knocked down all the pseudo-truths that years of "field studies" were believed to have amply confirmed. To be sure, the Algerian Revolution has brought about an objective modification of attitudes and outlook. But the Algerian people had never disarmed. November 1, 1954, was not the awakening of the people, but the signal it was waiting for in order to get into motion, in order to put into practice in full daylight a tactic acquired, and solidly reinforced, in the heyday of the Franco-Moslem period.

The Algerian woman, like her brothers, had minutely built up defense mechanisms which enable her today to play a primary role in the struggle for liberation.

To begin with, there is the much-discussed status of the Algerian woman—her alleged confinement, her lack of importance, her humility, her silent existence bordering on quasi-absence. And "Moslem society" has made no place for her, amputating her personality, allowing her neither development nor maturity, maintaining her in a perpetual infantilism.

Such affirmations, illuminated by "scientific works," are today receiving the only valid challenge: the experience of revolution.

The Algerian woman's ardent love of the home is not a limitation imposed by the universe. It is not hatred of the sun or the streets or spectacles. It is not a flight from the world.

What is true is that under normal conditions, an interaction must exist between the family and society at large. The home is the basis of the truth of society, but society authenticates and legitimizes the family. The colonial structure is the very negation of this reciprocal justification. The Algerian woman, in imposing such a restriction on herself, in choosing a form of existence limited in scope, was deepening her consciousness of struggle and preparing for combat.

This withdrawal, this rejection of an imposed structure, this falling back upon the fertile kernel that a restricted but coherent existence represents, constituted for a long time the fundamental strength of the occupied. All alone, the woman, by means of conscious techniques, presided over the setting up of the system. What was essential was that the occupier should constantly come up against a unified front. This accounts for the aspect of sclerosis that tradition must assume.

In reality, the effervescence and the revolutionary spirit have been kept alive by the woman in the home. For revolutionary war is not a war of men.

It is not a war waged with an active army and reserves. Revolutionary war, as the Algerian people is waging it, is a total war in which the woman does not merely knit for or mourn the soldier. The Algerian woman is at the heart of the combat. Arrested, tortured, raped, shot down, she testifies to the violence of the occupier and to his inhumanity.

As a nurse, a liaison agent, a fighter, she bears witness to the depth and the density of the struggle.

We shall speak also of the woman's fatalism, of her absence of reaction in the face of adversity, of her inability to measure the gravity of events. The constant smile, the persistence of an apparently unfounded hope, the refusal to go down on her knees, is likened to an inability to grasp reality.

The humor which is a rigorous appraisal of events is unperceived by the occupier. And the courage that the Algerian woman manifests in the struggle is not an unexpected creation or the result of a mutation. It is the insurrectional phase of that same humor.

The woman's place in Algerian society is indicated with such vehemence that the occupier's confusion is readily understandable. This is because Algerian society reveals itself not to be the womanless society that had been so convincingly described.

Side by side with us, our sisters do their part in further breaking down the enemy system and in liquidating the old mystifications once and for all.

2

This Is the Voice of Algeria

We propose in this chapter to study the new attitudes adopted by the Algerian people in the course of the fight for liberation, with respect to a precise technical instrument: the radio. We shall see that what is being called into question behind these new developments in Algerian life is the entire colonial situation. We shall have occasion to show throughout this book that the challenging of the very principle of foreign domination brings about essential mutations in the consciousness of the colonized, in the manner in which he perceives the colonizer, in his human status in the world.

Radio-Alger, the French broadcasting station which has been established in Algeria for decades, a re-edition or an echo of the French National Broadcasting System operating from Paris, is essentially the instrument of colonial society and its values. The great majority of Europeans in Algeria own receiving sets. Before 1945, 95 per cent of the receivers were in the hands of Europeans. The Algerians who owned radios belonged mainly to the "developed bourgeoisie," and included a number of Kabyles who had formerly emigrated and had since returned to their villages. The sharp economic stratification between the dominant and the dominated societies in large part explains this state of things. But naturally, as in every colonial situation, this category of realities takes on a specific coloration. Thus hundreds of Algerian families whose standard of living was sufficient to enable them to acquire a radio did not acquire one. Yet there was no rational decision to refuse this instrument. There was no organized resistance to this device. No real lines of counter-acculturation, such as are described in certain monographs devoted to underdeveloped regions, have been shown to exist, even after extensive surveys. It may be pointed out, nevertheless —and this argument may have appeared to confirm the conclusions of sociologists—that, pressed with questions as to the reasons for this reluctance, Algerians rather frequently give the following answer: "Traditions of respectability are so important for us and are so hierarchical, that it is practically impossible for us to listen to radio programs in the family. The sex allusions, or even the clownish situations meant to make people laugh, which are broadcast over the radio cause an unendurable strain in a family listening to these programs."

The ever possible eventuality of laughing in the presence of the head of the family or the elder brother, of listening in common to amorous words or terms of levity, obviously acts as a deterrent to the distribution of radios in Algerian native society. It is with reference to this first rationalization that we must understand the habit formed by the official Radio Broadcasting Services in Algeria of announcing the programs that can be listened to in common and those in the course of which the traditional forms of sociability might be too severely strained.

Here, then, at a certain explicit level, is the apprehension of a fact: receiving sets are not readily adopted by Algerian society. By and large, it refuses this technique which threatens its stability and the traditional types of sociability; the reason invoked being that the programs in Algeria, undifferentiated because they are copied from the Western model, are not adapted to the strict, almost feudal type of patrilineal hierarchy, with its many moral taboos, that characterizes the Algerian family.

On the basis of this analysis, techniques of approach could be proposed. Among others, the staggering of broadcasts addressed to the family as a whole, to male groups, to female groups, etc. As we describe the radical transformations that have occurred in this realm, in connection with the national war, we shall see how artificial such a sociological approach is, what a mass of errors it contains.

We have already noted the accelerated speed with which the radio was adopted by the European society. The introduction of the radio in the colonizing society proceeded at a rate comparable to that of the most developed Western regions. We must always remember that in the colonial situation, in which, as we have seen, the social dichotomy reaches an incomparable intensity, there is a frenzied and almost laughable growth of middle-class gentility on the part of the nationals from the metropolis. For a European to own a radio is of course to participate in the eternal round of Western petty-bourgeois ownership, which extends from the radio to the villa, including the car and the refrigerator. It also gives him the feeling that colonial society is a living and palpitating reality, with its festivities, its traditions eager to establish themselves, its progress, its taking root. But especially, in the hinterland, in the so-called colonization centers, it is the only link with the cities, with Algiers, with the metropolis, with the world of the civilized. It is one of the means of escaping the inert, passive, and sterilizing pressure of the "native" environment. It is, according to the settler's expression, "the only way to still feel like a civilized man."

On the farms, the radio reminds the settler of the reality of colonial power and, by its very existence, dispenses safety, serenity. Radio-Alger is a confirmation of the settler's right and strengthens his certainty in the historic continuity of the conquest, hence of his farm. The Paris music, extracts from the metropolitan press, the French government crises, constitute a coherent background from which colonial society draws its density and its justification. Radio-Alger sustains the occupant's culture, marks it off from the non-culture, from the nature of the occupied. Radio-Alger, the voice of France in Algeria, constitutes the sole center of reference at the level of news. Radio-Alger, for the settler, is a daily invitation not to "go native," not to forget the rightfulness of his culture. The settlers in the remote outposts, the pioneering adventurers, are well aware of this when they say that "without wine and the radio, we should already have become Arabized."[1]

In Algeria, before 1945, the radio as a technical news instrument became widely distributed in the dominant society. It then, as we have seen, became both a means of resistance in the case of isolated Europeans and a means of cultural pressure on the dominated society. Among European farmers, the radio was broadly regarded as a link with the civilized world, as an effective instrument of resistance to the corrosive influence of an inert native society, of a society without a future, backward and devoid of value.

For the Algerian, however, the situation was totally different. We have seen that the more well-to-do family hesitated to buy a radio set. Yet no explicit, organized, and motivated resistance was to be observed, but rather a dull absence of interest in that piece of French presence. In rural areas and in regions remote from the colonization centers, the situation was clearer. There no one was faced with the problem, or rather, the problem was so remote from the everyday concerns of the native that it was quite clear to an inquirer that it would be outrageous to ask an Algerian why he did not own a radio.

A man conducting a survey during this period who might be looking for satisfactory answers would find himself unable to obtain the information he needed. All the pretexts put forth had of course to be carefully weighed. At the level of actual experience, one cannot expect to obtain a rationalization of attitudes and choices.

Two levels of explanation can be suggested here. As an instrumental technique in the limited sense, the radio receiving set develops the sensorial, intellectual, and muscular powers of man in a given society. *The radio in occupied Algeria is a technique in the hands of the occupier which, within the framework of colonial domination, corresponds to no vital need insofar as*

[1] Radio-Alger is in fact one of the mooring-lines maintained by the dominant society. Radio-Monte-Carlo, Radio-Paris, Radio-Andorre likewise play a protective role against "Arabization."

the "native" is concerned. The radio, as a symbol of French presence, as a material representation of the colonial configuration, is characterized by an extremely important negative valence. The possible intensification and extension of sensorial or intellectual powers by the French radio are implicitly rejected or denied by the native. The technical instrument, the new scientific acquisitions, when they contain a sufficient charge to threaten a given feature of the native society, are never perceived in themselves, in calm objectivity. The technical instrument is rooted in the colonial situation where, as we know, the negative or positive coefficients always exist in a very accentuated way.

At another level, as a system of information, as a bearer of language, hence of message, the radio may be apprehended within the colonial situation in a special way. Radiophonic technique, the press, and in a general way the systems, messages, sign transmitters, exist in colonial society in accordance with a well-defined statute. Algerian society, the dominated society, never participates in this world of signs. The messages broadcast by Radio-Alger are listened to solely by the representatives of power in Algeria, solely by the members of the dominant authority and seem magically to be avoided by the members of the "native" society. The non-acquisition of receiver sets by this society has precisely the effect of strengthening this impression of a closed and privileged world that characterizes colonialist news. In the matter of daily programs, before 1954, eulogies addressed to the occupation troops were certainly largely absent. From time to time, to be sure, there might be an evocation over the radio of the outstanding dates of the conquest of Algeria, in the course of which, with an almost unconscious obscenity, the occupier would belittle and humiliate the Algerian resistant of 1830. There were also the commemorative celebrations in which the "Moslem" veterans would be invited to place a wreath at the foot of the statue of General Bugeaud or of Sergeant Blandan, both heroes of the conquest and liquidators of thousands of Algerian patriots. But on the whole it could not be said that the clearly racialist or anti-Algerian content accounted for the indifference and the resistance of the native. *The explanation seems rather to be that Radio-Alger is regarded by the Algerian as the spokesman of the colonial world. Before the war the Algerian, with his own brand of humor, had defined Radio-Alger as "Frenchmen speaking to Frenchmen."*

1945 was to bring Algeria abruptly onto the international scene. For weeks, the 45,000 victims of Sétif and of Guelma[2] were matter for abundant comment in the newspapers and information bulletins of regions until then unaware of or indifferent to the fate of Algeria. The tragedy of their dead or mutilated brothers and the fervent sympathy conveyed to them by men and women in America, Europe, and Africa left a deep mark on the Algerians themselves, foreshadowing more fundamental changes. The awakening of the colonial world and the progressive liberation of peoples long held in subjection involved Algeria in a process which reached beyond her and of which, at the same time, she became a part. The appearance of liberated Arab countries at this point is of exceptional importance. The first wholesale introduction of radio sets in Algeria coincided with the setting up of national broadcasting stations in Syria, Egypt and Lebanon.

After 1947-1948, the number of radios grew, but at a moderate rate. Even then, the Algerian when he turned on his radio was interested exclusively in foreign and Arab broadcasts. Radio-Alger was listened to only because it broadcast typically Algerian music, national music. In the face of this budding Algerian market, European agencies began to look for "native" representatives. The European firms were now convinced that the sale of radio sets depended on the nationality of the dealer. Algerian intermediaries were increasingly solicited for the handling of radios. This innovation in the distribution system was

[2] Sétif and Guelma—two central points in a Moslem uprising that occurred in the region of Kabylia in May 1945. In the repression, which lasted some two weeks, aviation and artillery took a heavy toll of lives. (Translator's note)

accompanied by an intensification of the marketing of these sets. It was during this period that a certain part of the Algerian lower middle class became owners of radios.

But it was in 1951-1952, at the time of the first skirmishes in Tunisia, that the Algerian people felt it necessary to increase their news network. In 1952-1953 Morocco undertook its war of liberation, and on November 1, 1954, Algeria joined the anti-colonialist Maghreb Front. It was precisely at this time, while radio sets were being acquired, that the most important development occurred in the defining of new attitudes to this specific technique for the dissemination of news.

It was from the occupiers' reactions that the Algerian learned that something grave and important was happening in his country. The European, through the triple network of the press, the radio and his travels, had a fairly clear idea of the dangers threatening colonial society. The Algerian who read in the occupier's face the increasing bankruptcy of colonialism felt the compelling and vital need to be informed. The vague impression that something fundamental was happening was strengthened both by the solemn decision of the patriots which expressed the secret yearning of the people and which embodied the determination, still devoid of content even yesterday, to exist as a nation, and more especially by the objective and visible crumbling away of the settler's serenity.

The struggle for liberation, reflected in the settler's sudden affability or in his unexpected, unmotivated bursts of temper, obliged the Algerian to follow the evolution of the confrontation step by step. In this period of setting up the lines of conflict, the Europeans committed many errors. Thus on the farms, settlers would assemble agricultural workers to announce to them that a given "gang of rebels," which was in fact unknown to the region, had been decimated in the Aurès Mountains or in Kabylia. At other times the servants would be offered a bottle of lemonade or a slice of cake because three or four suspects had just been executed a few kilometers from the property.

From the first months of the Revolution the Algerian, with a view to self-protection and in order to escape what he considered to be the occupier's lying maneuvers, thus found himself having to acquire his own source of information. It became essential to know what was going on, to be informed both of the enemy's real losses and his own. The Algerian at this time had to bring his life up to the level of the Revolution. He had to enter the vast network of news; he had to find his way in a world in which things happened, in which events existed, in which forces were active. Through the experience of a war waged by his own people, the Algerian came in contact with an active community. The Algerian found himself having to oppose the enemy news with his own news. The "truth" of the oppressor, formerly rejected as an absolute lie, was now countered by another, an acted truth. The occupier's lie thereby acquired greater reality, for it was now a menaced lie, put on the defensive. It was the defenses of the occupier, his reactions, his resistances, that underscored the effectiveness of national action and made that action participate in a world of truth. The Algerian's reaction was no longer one of pained and desperate refusal. *Because it avowed its own uneasiness, the occupier's lie became a positive aspect of the nation's new truth.*

During the first months of the war, it was by means of the press that the Algerian attempted to organize his own news distribution system. The democratic press still existing in Algeria and the newspapers with an anti-colonialist tradition or a policy of objectivity were then avidly read by the native. It was in this sector of news distribution that the Algerian found balance-restoring elements. The power of the colonialist message, the systems used to impose it and present it as *the truth* were such that most of the time the colonized had only his own increasingly overshadowed inner conviction to oppose to the eminently traumatizing offensives of the French press and the spectacular manifestations of the military and police power. Confronted daily with "the wiping out of the last remaining guerrilla bands," the civilian could fight off despair only by an act of faith, by an obstinate belief.

Progressively the moral (because objective) support provided by the democratic press ceased. The self-censorship of the local newspapers known for their traditional honesty strengthened this impression of incompleteness, of sketchiness, even of betrayal in the realm of news. It seemed to the Algerian that whole sections of truth were hidden from him. He felt the near-certainty that the colonialist power was crumbling before his eyes and that the progress of its dissolution was being kept from him. He fell prey to the sudden fear that this thing, so often hated, wounded to the death in the *djebel,* its days probably numbered, would disappear without his being able to see at close hand its power and its arrogance in the process of disintegration. During this period the Algerian experienced a sense of frustration. His aggressiveness remained in suspense because he could not keep the score, because he could not register the setbacks of the enemy hour by hour, because, finally, he could not measure centimeter by centimeter the progressive shrinking of the occupying power.

The European, on the whole, sized up the dimensions of the rebellion rather objectively. He did not really believe that some fine morning the revolutionary troops would take over in the city. But he knew more or less precisely how great the forces of the Revolution were and he was constantly comparing them with those represented by the French troops. Every plane that streaked the sky, every armored tank advancing in the dawn were as many spots of sunlight in the settler's anxious and uncertain world. The European felt the shock, but in those first months of 1955 he believed that nothing was lost, that there was still a future for colonialism in Algeria. The official statements of the radio strengthened him in this position. The Algerian, on the other hand, especially if he lived in the rural areas, supplemented his absence of news by an absolutely irrational overestimation. Reactions occurred at that time which were so disproportionate to objective reality that to an observer they assumed a pathological character. In the first months of 1955 there were rumors in Constantine to the effect that Algiers, for example, was in the hands of the nationalists, or in Algiers that the Algerian flag was hoisted over Constantine, Philippeville, Batna. . . .

In the small colonization centers the settlers could not always understand the *fellah's* fierce and sudden assurance, and there were times when they would telephone to the nearest city, only to have it confirmed that nothing unusual had happened in the country. The European became aware of the fact that the life he had built on the agony of the colonized people was losing its assurance.

Before the rebellion there was the life, the movement, the existence of the settler, and on the other side the continued agony of the colonized. Since 1954, the European has discovered that another life parallel to his own has begun to stir, and that in Algerian society, it seems, things no longer repeat themselves as they did before. The European, after 1954, knew that something was being hidden from him. This is the period in which the old pejorative expression, *the Arab telephone,* has taken on an almost scientific meaning.

In the Maghreb country, the Europeans use the term *Arab telephone* in speaking of the relative speed with which news travels by word of mouth in the native society. Never at any time was the expression intended to mean anything else. But in 1955 Europeans, and even Algerians, could be heard to refer confidentially, and as though revealing a state secret, to a technique of long-distance communication that vaguely recalled some such system of signaling, like the tom-tom, as is found in certain regions of Africa. The Algerian gave the isolated European the impression of being in permanent contact with the revolutionary high command. He showed a kind of amplified self-assurance which assumed rather extraordinary forms. There were cases of real "running amuck."

Individuals in a fit of aberration would lose control of themselves. They would be seen dashing down a street or into an isolated farm, unarmed, or waving a miserable jagged knife, shouting, "Long live independent Algeria! We've won!" This aggressive kind of behavior, which assumed violent forms, would usually end in a burst of machine-gun bullets fired by a patrol. When a doctor was able to exchange words with one of these dying men, the usual kind of expression he heard would be something like, "Don't believe them! We've got the upper edge, our men are coming, I've been sent to tell you they're coming! We're powerful and we'll smash the enemy!"

These hysterical cases were sometimes merely wounded and were given over to the police for questioning. The pathological nature of their behavior would not be recognized, and the accused would be tortured for days until the press reported that he had been shot trying to escape while being transferred to another prison, or that he had died of a recurring ailment. In the dominant group, likewise, there were cases of mental hysteria; people would be seized with a collective fear and panicky settlers were seen to seek an outlet in criminal acts. What made the two cases different was that, unlike the colonized, the colonizer always translated his subjective states into acts, real and multiple murders. We propose to deal with these different problems, arising out of the struggle for liberation, in a study directly based on psychopathology, its forms, its original features, its description.

On the level of news, the Algerian was to find himself caught in a network strictly confined in space. In a village everyone is informed as to the numerical size and the equipment of the National Army of Liberation. On request, information as to its striking power and plan of operations can be obtained. No one, of course, can give the source of such information, but the reliability is unchallengeable. The description that has been given, when a national army collapses, of the rapidity with which alarming, catastrophic, disastrous news spreads among the people can serve as a system of reference to appraise the opposite phenomenon. In 1940 segments of a Fifth Column may have been discovered which were assigned to inoculate the French people with the virus of defeat, but it must not be overlooked that the ground was already prepared, that there was a kind of spiritual demobilization, due to the setbacks suffered by democracy in Spain, in Italy, in Germany, and especially at Munich. The defeatism of 1940 was the direct product of the defeatism of Munich.

In Algeria, on the contrary—and this is true for all colonial countries that undertake a national war—all the news is good, every bit of information is gratifying. The Fifth Column is an impossibility in Algeria. It is the recognition of this fact that leads sociologists to rediscover the old explanation according to which the "native" is inaccessible to reason or to experience. War specialists observe more empirically that these men have an iron morale or that their fanaticism is incomprehensible. The group considered as a whole gives the impression of supplementing what it gets in the way of news by an assurance more and more cut off from reality. These manifestations, these attitudes of total belief, this collective conviction, express the determination of the group to get as close as possible to the Revolution, to get ahead of the Revolution if possible, in short *to be in on it.*

At the same time, as we have seen, especially in the urban centers, more complex patterns of behavior came to light. Avid for objective news, the Algerians would buy the democratic papers that arrived from France. This meant an undeniable financial benefit for these papers. *L'Express, France-Observateur, Le Monde* increased their sales three- and even five-fold in Algeria. The men running newspaper kiosks, almost all of them Europeans, were the first to point out the economic, and secondarily the political danger that these publications represented. In studying the problem of the press in Algeria, one must always bear in mind one peculiarity in the distribution system. The public criers, all young Algerians, sell only the local press. The European papers are not brought to the consumer. These papers have to be bought at the kiosks. The owners of the Algerian press immediately feel the competition of the press coming from France. Campaigns denouncing the press for being "in cahoots with the enemy," and the repeated seizures of a certain number of these publications obviously assumed a special meaning. More and more newsdealers, when asked for these papers, would reply aggressively that the "s.o.b. papers haven't arrived today."

Algerians in the cities, but especially in the rural centers, then discovered that showing concern over the arrival or non-arrival of the said press was sufficient to label them. In Algeria as in France, but of course more markedly, the newspaper kiosk dealer, like the office clerk, is sure to be a veteran with strong backing in ultra-colonialist circles. For the Algerian to ask for *L'Express, L'Humanité,* or *Le Monde* was tantamount to publicly confessing—as likely as not to a police informer—his allegiance to the Revolution; it was in any case an unguarded indication that he had reservations as to the official, or "colonialist" news; it meant manifesting his willingness to make himself conspicuous; for the kiosk dealer it was the unqualified affirmation by that Algerian of solidarity with the Revolution. The purchase of such a newspaper was thus considered to be a nationalist act. Hence it quickly became a dangerous act.

Every time the Algerian asked for one of these newspapers, the kiosk dealer, who represented the occupier, would regard it as an expression of nationalism, equivalent to an act of war. Because they were now really committed to activities vital to the Revolution, or out of understandable prudence, if one bears in mind the wave of xenophobia created by the French settlers in 1955, Algerian adults soon formed the habit of getting young Algerians to buy these newspapers. It took only a few weeks for this new "trick" to be discovered. After a certain period the newsdealers refused to sell *L'Express, L'Humanité,* and *Libération* to minors. Adults were then reduced to coming out into the open or else to falling back on *L'Echo d'Alger.* It was at this point that the political directorate of the Revolution gave orders to boycott the Algerian local press.

This decision had a double objective. First, to counter the offensive of the Algerian trusts by a measure having economic consequences. By depriving the Algerian papers of a large proportion of their native customers the revolutionary movement was dealing a rather effective blow to the market of the local press. But above all, the political directorate was convinced that, having to depend solely on colonialist news, the Algerians would gradually succumb to the massive and baneful influence of those pages in which figures and photographs were complacently displayed and where in any case one could clearly read every morning about the elimination of the Revolution.

On the level of the masses, which had remained relatively uninvolved in the struggle since they couldn't read the press, the necessity of having radio sets was felt. It must not be forgotten that the people's generalized illiteracy left it indifferent to things written. In the first months of the Revolution, the great majority of Algerians identified everything written in the French language as the expression of colonial domination. The language in which *L'Express* and *L'Echo d'Alger* were written was the sign of the French presence.

The acquisition of a radio set in Algeria, in 1955, represented the sole means of obtaining news of the Revolution from non-French sources. This necessity assumed a compelling character when the people learned that there were Algerians in Cairo who daily drew up the balance-sheet of the liberation struggle. From Cairo, from Syria, from nearly all the Arab countries, the great pages written in the *djebels* by brothers, relatives, friends flowed back to Algeria.

Meanwhile, despite these new occurrences, the introduction of radio sets into houses and the most remote *douars* proceeded only gradually. There was no enormous rush to buy receivers.

It was at the end of 1956 that the real shift occurred. At this time tracts were distributed announcing the existence of a Voice of Free Algeria. The broadcasting schedules and the wavelengths were given. This voice "that speaks from the *djebels*," not geographically limited, but bringing to all Algeria the great message of the Revolution, at once acquired an essential value. In less than twenty days the entire stock of radio sets was bought up. In the *souks*[3] trade in used receiver sets began. Algerians who had served their apprenticeship with European radio-electricians opened small shops. Moreover, the dealers had to meet new needs. The absence of electrification in immense regions in Algeria naturally created special problems for the consumer. For this reason battery-operated receivers, from 1956 on, were in great demand on Algerian territory. In a few weeks several thousand sets were sold to Algerians, who bought them as individuals, families, groups of houses, *douars, mechtas.*

Since 1956 the purchase of a radio in Algeria has meant, not the adoption of a modern technique for getting news, but the obtaining of access to the only means of entering into communication with the Revolution, of living with it. In the special case of the portable battery set, an improved form of the standard receiver operating on current, the specialist in technical changes in underdeveloped countries might see a sign of a radical mutation. The Algerian, in fact, gives the impression of finding short cuts and of achieving the most modern forms of news-communication without passing through the intermediary stages.[4] In reality, we have seen that this "progress" is to be explained by the absence of electric current in the Algerian *douars.*

The French authorities did not immediately realize the exceptional importance of this change in attitude of the Algerian people with regard to the radio. Traditional resistances broke down and one could see in a *douar* groups of families in which fathers, mothers, daughters, elbow to elbow, would scrutinize the radio dial waiting for the *Voice of Algeria.* Suddenly indifferent to the sterile, archaic modesty and antique social arrangements devoid of brotherhood, the Algerian family discovered itself to be immune to the off-color jokes and the libidinous references that the announcer occasionally let drop.

[3] *souk*—market or shop. (Translator's note)

[4] In the realm of military communications, the same phenomenon is to be noted. In less than fifteen months the National Army of Liberation's "liaison and telecommunications system" became equal to the best that is to be found in a modern army.

Almost magically—but we have seen the rapid and dialectical progression of the new national requirements—the technical instrument of the radio receiver lost its identity as an enemy object. The radio set was no longer a part of the occupier's arsenal of cultural oppression. In making of the radio a primary means of resisting the increasingly overwhelming psychological and military pressures of the occupant, Algerian society made an autonomous decision to embrace the new technique and thus tune itself in on the new signaling systems brought into being by the Revolution.

The Voice of Fighting Algeria was to be of capital importance in consolidating and unifying the people. We shall see that the use of the Arab, Kabyle and French languages which, as colonialism was obliged to recognize, was the expression of a non-racial conception, had the advantage of developing and of strengthening the unity of the people, of making the fighting Djurdjura area real for the Algerian patriots of Batna or of Nemours. The fragments and splinters of acts gleaned by the correspondent of a newspaper more or less attached to the colonial domination, or communicated by the opposing military authorities, lost their anarchic character and became organized into a national and Algerian political idea, assuming their place in an overall strategy of the reconquest of the people's sovereignty. The scattered acts fitted into a vast epic, and the Kabyles were no longer "the men of the mountains," but the brothers who with Ouamrane and Krim made things difficult for the enemy troops.

Having a radio meant paying one's taxes to the nation, buying the right of entry into the struggle of an assembled people.

The French authorities, however, began to realize the importance of this progress of the people in the technique of news dissemination. After a few months of hesitancy legal measures appeared. The sale of radios was now prohibited, except on presentation of a voucher issued by the military security or police services. The sale of battery sets was absolutely prohibited, and spare batteries were practically withdrawn from the market. The Algerian dealers now had the opportunity to put their patriotism to the test, and they were able to supply the people with spare batteries with exemplary regularity by resorting to various subterfuges.[5]

The Algerian who wanted to live up to the Revolution, had at last the possibility of hearing an official voice, the voice of the combatants, explain the combat to him, tell him the story of the Liberation on the march, and incorporate it into the nation's new life.

Here we come upon a phenomenon that is sufficiently unusual to retain our attention. The highly trained French services, rich with experience acquired in modern wars, past masters in the practice of "sound-wave warfare," were quick to detect the wave lengths of the broadcasting stations. The programs were then systematically jammed, and the *Voice of Fighting Algeria* soon became inaudible. A new form of struggle had come into being. Tracts were distributed telling the Algerians to keep tuned in for a period of two or three hours. In the course of a single broadcast a second station, broadcasting over a different wave-length, would relay the first jammed station. The listener, enrolled in the battle of the waves, had to figure out the tactics of the enemy, and in an almost physical way circumvent the strategy of the adversary. Very often only the operator, his ear glued to the receiver, had the unhoped-for opportunity of hearing the *Voice*. The other Algerians present in the room would receive the echo of this voice through the privileged interpreter who, at the end of the broadcast, was literally besieged. Specific questions would then be asked of this incarnated voice. Those present wanted to know about a particular battle mentioned by the French press in the last twenty-four hours, and the inter-

[5] The arrival in Algeria by normal channels of new sets and new batteries obviously became increasingly difficult. After 1957 it was from Tunisia and Morocco, via the underground, that new supplies came. The regular introduction of these means of establishing contact with the official voice of the Revolution became as important for the people as acquiring weapons or munitions for the National Army.

preter, embarrassed, feeling guilty, would sometimes have to admit that the *Voice* had not mentioned it.

But by common consent, after an exchange of views, it would be decided that the *Voice* had in fact spoken of these events, but that the interpreter had not caught the transmitted information. A real task of reconstruction would then begin. Everyone would participate, and the battles of yesterday and the day before would be re-fought in accordance with the deep aspirations and the unshakable faith of the group. The listener would compensate for the fragmentary nature of the news by an autonomous creation of information.

Listening to the *Voice of Fighting Algeria* was motivated not just by eagerness to hear the news, but more particularly by the inner need to be at one with the nation in its struggle, to recapture and to assume the new national formulation, to listen to and to repeat the grandeur of the epic being accomplished up there among the rocks and on the *djebels*. Every morning the Algerian would communicate the result of his hours of listening in. Every morning he would complete for the benefit of his neighbor or his comrade the things not said by the *Voice* and reply to the insidious questions asked by the enemy press. He would counter the official affirmations of the occupier, the resounding bulletins of the adversary, with official statements issued by the Revolutionary Command.

Sometimes it was the militant who would circulate the assumed point of view of the political directorate. Because of a silence on this or that fact which, if prolonged, might prove upsetting and dangerous for the people's unity, the whole nation would snatch fragments of sentences in the course of a broadcast and attach to them a decisive meaning. Imperfectly heard, obscured by an incessant jamming, forced to change wave lengths two or three times in the course of a broadcast, the *Voice of Fighting Algeria* could hardly ever be heard from beginning to end. It was a choppy, broken voice. From one village to the next, from one shack to the next, the *Voice of Algeria* would recount new things, tell of more and more glorious battles, picture vividly the collapse of the occupying power. The enemy lost its density, and at the level of the consciousness of the occupied, experienced a series of essential setbacks. Thus the *Voice of Algeria,* which for months led the life of a fugitive, which was tracked by the adversary's powerful jamming networks, and whose "word" was often inaudible, nourished the citizen's faith in the Revolution.

This *Voice* whose presence was felt, whose reality was sensed, assumed more and more weight in proportion to the number of jamming wave lengths broadcast by the specialized enemy stations. It was the power of the enemy sabotage that emphasized the reality and the intensity of the national expression. By its phantom-like character, the radio of the *Moudjahidines,* speaking in the name of Fighting Algeria, recognized as the spokesman for every Algerian, gave to the combat its maximum of reality.

Under these conditions, claiming to have heard the *Voice of Algeria* was, in a certain sense, distorting the truth, but it was above all the occasion to proclaim one's clandestine participation in the essence of the Revolution. It meant making a deliberate choice, though it was not explicit during the first months, between the enemy's congenital lie and the people's own lie, which suddenly acquired a dimension of truth.

This voice, often absent, physically inaudible, which each one felt welling up within himself, founded on an inner perception of the Fatherland, became materialized in an irrefutable way. Every Algerian, for his part, broadcast and transmitted the new language. The nature of this voice recalled in more than one way that of the Revolution: present "in the air" in isolated pieces, but not objectively.[6]

The radio receiver guaranteed this true lie. Every evening,

[6] Along the same line should be mentioned the manner in which programs are listened to in Kabylia. In groups of scores and sometimes hundreds around a receiver, the peasants listen religiously to "the Voice of the Arabs." Few understand the literary Arabic used in these broadcasts. But the faces assume a look of gravity and the features harden when the expression *Istiqlal* (Independence) resounds in the *gourbi* (shack). An Arab voice that hammers out the word *Istiqlal* four times in an hour suffices at that level of heightened consciousness to keep alive the faith in victory.

from nine o'clock to midnight, the Algerian would listen. At the end of the evening, not hearing the *Voice,* the listener would sometimes leave the needle on a jammed wave-length or one that simply produced static, and would announce that the voice of the combatants was here. For an hour the room would be filled with the piercing, excruciating din of the jamming. Behind each modulation, each active crackling, the Algerian would imagine not only words, but concrete battles. The war of the sound waves, in the *gourbi,* re-enacts for the benefit of the citizen the armed clash of his people and colonialism. As a general rule, it is the *Voice of Algeria* that wins out. The enemy stations, once the broadcast is completed, abandon their work of sabotage. The military music of warring Algeria that concludes the broadcast can then freely fill the lungs and the heads of the faithful. These few brazen notes reward three hours of daily hope and have played a fundamental role for months in the training and strengthening of the Algerian national consciousness.

On the psychopathological level, it is important to mention a few phenomena pertaining to the radio which made their appearance in connection with the war of liberation. Before 1954, the monographs written on Algerians suffering from hallucinations constantly pointed out the presence in the so-called "external action phase" of highly aggressive and hostile radio voices. These metallic, cutting, insulting, disagreeable voices all have for the Algerian an accusing, inquisitorial character. The radio, on the normal level, already apprehended as an instrument of the occupation, as a type of violent invasion on the part of the oppressor, assumes highly alienating meanings in the field of the pathological. The radio, in addition to the somewhat irrational magical elements with which it is invested in the majority of homogeneous societies, that is to say societies from which all foreign oppression is absent, has a particular valence in Algeria. We have seen that the voice heard is not indifferent, is not neutral; it is the voice of the oppressor, the voice of the enemy. The speech delivered is not received, deciphered, understood, but rejected. The communication is never questioned, but is simply refused, for it is precisely the opening of oneself to the other that is organically excluded from the colonial situation. Before 1954, in the psychopathological realm, the radio was an evil object, anxiogenic and accursed.

After 1954, the radio assumed totally new meanings. The phenomena of the wireless and the receiver set lost their coefficient of hostility, were stripped of their character of extraneousness, and became part of the coherent order of the nation in battle. In hallucinatory psychoses, after 1956, the radio voices became protective, friendly. Insults and accusations disappeared and gave way to words of encouragement. The foreign technique, which had been "digested" in connection with the national struggle, had become a fighting instrument for the people and a protective organ against anxiety.[7]

Still on the level of communication, attention must be called to the acquisition of new values by the French language. The French language, language of occupation, a vehicle of the oppressing power, seemed doomed for eternity to judge the Algerian in a pejorative way. Every French expression referring to the Algerian had a humiliating content. Every French speech heard was an order, a threat, or an insult. The contact between the Algerian and the European is defined by these three spheres. The broadcasting in French of the programs of *Fighting Algeria* was to liberate the enemy language from its historic meanings. The same message transmitted in three different languages unified the experience and gave it a universal dimension. The French language lost its accursed character, revealing itself to be capable also of transmitting, for the benefit of the nation, the messages of truth that the latter awaited. Paradoxical as it may appear, it is the Algerian Revolution, it is the

[7] The appearance of themes of morbid protection, their importance as a technique of self-defense and even of self-cure in the historic development of mental disease, have already been studied in classic psychiatry. Plagued by his accusing "voices," the victim of hallucinations has no other recourse but to create friendly voices. This mechanism of transformation into its antithesis that we here point out has its counterpart in the disintegrating colonial situation.

struggle of the Algerian people, that is facilitating the spreading of the French language in the nation.

In psychopathology, sentences in French lose their automatic character of insult and malediction. When they hear French voices, Algerians suffering from hallucinations quote words that are less and less aggressive. It is not uncommon, at a later stage, to note that hallucinations in the language of the occupier assume a friendly character of support, of protection.[8]

The occupation authorities have not measured the importance of the new attitude of the Algerian toward the French language. Expressing oneself in French, understanding French, was no longer tantamount to treason or to an impoverishing identification with the occupier. Used by the *Voice of the Combatants,* conveying in a positive way the message of the Revolution, the French language also becomes an instrument of liberation. Whereas formerly, in psychopathology, any French voice, to one in a delirium, expressed rejection, condemnation and opprobrium, with the struggle for liberation we see the initiation of a major process of exorcizing the French language. The "native" can almost be said to assume responsibility for the language of the occupier.[9]

It was after the *Congress of the Soummam,* in August 1956, that the French became aware of this phenomenon. It will be remembered that on this occasion, the political and military leaders of the Revolution met in the *Valley of the Soummam,* precisely in the sector of Amirouche, the then Commander, to lay the doctrinal foundations of the struggle and to set up the *National Council of the Algerian Revolution* (CNRA). The fact that the discussions were carried on in French suddenly

[8] What is involved here is not the emergence of an ambivalence, but rather a mutation, a radical change of valence, not a back-and-forth movement but a dialectical progression.

[9] On the other hand, the *Voice of Algeria* was imagined to be pronouncing death sentences by certain Algerian collaborators. Suffering from serious fits of depression, these men who usually belonged to the police services, would be attacked, insulted, convicted by the "rebel" radio. Likewise, European women as well as European men in outbreaks of anxiety would very clearly hear threats or condemnations in the Arabic language. Such phenomena were practically unknown before 1954.

revealed to the occupation forces that the traditional general reticence of the Algerian with regard to using French within the colonial situation might no longer exist, when a decisive confrontation brought the will to national independence of the people and the dominant power face to face.

The French authorities were curiously baffled by this phenomenon. They first saw in it the proof of what they had always claimed—i.e., the incapacity of the Arabic language to handle the operational concepts of a modern revolutionary war. But at the same time, the decisions reached in the occupier's linguistic system forced the occupier to realize the relative character of his signs and created confusion and disorder in his defense system.

The advocates of integration, for their part, here saw a new opportunity to promote a "French Algeria" by making the occupier's language the sole practical means of communication available to Kabyles, Arabs, Chaouias, Mozabites, etc. This thesis, on the level of language, went back to the very basis of colonialism: it is the intervention of the foreign nation that puts order into the original anarchy of the colonized country. Under these conditions, the French language, the language of the occupier, was given the role of *Logos,* with ontological implications within Algerian society.

In either case, using the French language was at the same time domesticating an attribute of the occupier and proving oneself open to the signs, the symbols, in short to a certain influence of the occupier. The French have not made a sufficiently thorough study of this new behavior of the Algerian with regard to their language. Before 1954, most of the work of the congresses of the nationalist parties was carried on in Arabic. More precisely, the militants of Kabylia or the Aurès would learn Arabic in connection with their national activities. Before 1954, speaking Arabic, refusing French as a language and as a means of cultural oppression, was a distinct and daily form of differentiation, of national existence. Before 1954, the nationalist parties sustained the hope of the militants and developed the political consciousness of the people by singling out and explaining, one by one, the value of the different configurations, the different characteristics of the occupied nation. The Arabic language was the most effective means that the *nation's being* had of unveiling itself.[10]

In August 1956, the reality of combat and the confusion of the occupier stripped the Arabic language of its sacred character, and the French language of its negative connotations. The new language of the nation could then make itself known through multiple meaningful channels.

The radio receiver as a technique of disseminating news and the French language as a basis for a possible communication became almost simultaneously accepted by the fighting nation.

We have seen that with the creation of the *Voice of Fighting Algeria,* radio sets multiplied to an extraordinary degree. Before 1954, the receiving instrument, the radiophonic technique of long-distance communication of thought was not, in Algeria, a mere neutral object. Looked upon as a transmission belt of the colonialist power, as a means in the hands of the occupier by which to maintain his strangle hold on the nation, the radio was frowned upon. Before 1954, switching on the radio meant giving asylum to the occupier's words; it meant allowing the colonizer's language to filter into the very heart of the house, the last of the supreme bastions of the national spirit. Before 1954, a radio in an Algerian house was the mark of Europeanization in progress, of vulnerability. It was the conscious opening to the influence of the dominator, to his pressure. It was the decision to *give voice to the occupier.* Having a radio meant accepting being besieged from within by the colonizer. It meant demonstrating that one chose cohabitation within the colonial frame-

[10] At the same period the political directorate decided to destroy the French radio in Algeria. The existence of a national voice led the heads of the movement to contemplate silencing Radio-Alger. Considerable damage was inflicted on technical facilities by the explosion of time bombs. But the broadcasts were soon resumed.

work. It meant, beyond any doubt, surrendering to the occupier.

We have mentioned the reasons invoked by the people to explain their reticence with respect to the radio. The desire to keep intact the traditional forms of sociability and the hierarchy of the family was then the main justification.

"We never know what program we are going to pick up." "There's no telling what they're going to say next." Sometimes a religious argument of a peremptory nature appears: "It's the infidels' radio." We have seen that such rationalizations are arbitrarily created to justify the rejection of the occupier's presence.

With the creation of a *Voice of Fighting Algeria,* the Algerian was vitally committed to listening to the message, to assimilating it, and soon to acting upon it. Buying a radio, getting down on one's knees with one's head against the speaker, was no longer just wanting to get the news concerning the formidable experience in progress in the country, it was *hearing* the first words of the nation.

Since the new Algeria on the march had decided to tell about itself and to make itself heard, the radio had become indispensable. It was the radio that enabled the *Voice* to take root in the villages and on the hills. Having a radio seriously meant *going to war.*

By means of the radio, a technique rejected before 1954, the Algerian people decided to relaunch the Revolution. Listening in on the Revolution, the Algerian existed with it, made it exist.

The memory of the "free" radios that came into being during the Second World War underlines the unique quality of the *Voice of Fighting Algeria.* The Polish, Belgian, French people, under the German occupation, were able, through the broadcasts transmitted from London, to maintain contact with a certain image of their nation. Hope, the spirit of resistance to the oppressor, were then given daily sustenance and kept alive. For example, it will be remembered that listening to the voice of

Free France was a mode of national existence, a form of combat. The fervent and well-nigh mystical participation of the French people with the voice from London has been sufficiently commented upon to need no amplification. In France, from 1940 to 1944, listening to the voice of *Free France* was surely a vital, sought-for experience. But listening to the radio was not a new phenomenon of behavior. The voice from London had its place in the vast repertory of transmitting stations which already existed for the French before the war. From the global conflict, a pre-eminent figure emerges through the agency—that of occupied France receiving the message of hope from *Free France*. In Algeria things took on a special character. First of all, there was the stripping from the instrument its traditional burden of taboos and prohibitions. Progressively the instrument not only acquired a category of neutrality, but was endowed with a positive coefficient.

Accepting the radio technique, buying a receiver set, and participating in the life of the fighting nation, all these coincided. The frenzy with which the people exhausted the stock of radio sets gives a rather accurate idea of its desire to be involved in the dialogue that began in 1955 between the combatant and the *nation*.

In the colonial society, Radio-Alger was not just one among a number of voices. *It was the voice of the occupier.* Tuning in Radio-Alger amounted to accepting domination; it amounted to exhibiting one's desire to live on good terms with oppression. It meant giving in to the enemy. Switching on the radio meant validating the formula, "This is Algiers, the French Radio Broadcast." The acquiring of a radio handed the colonized over to the enemy's system and prepared for the banishing of hope from his heart.

The existence of the *Voice of Fighting Algeria,* on the other hand, profoundly changed the problem. Every Algerian felt himself to be called upon and wanted to become a reverberating element of the vast network of meanings born of the liberating combat. The war, daily events of military or political character, were broadly commented on in the news programs of the foreign radios. In the foreground the voice of the *djebels* stood out. We have seen that the phantom-like and quickly inaudible character of this voice in no way affected *its felt reality and its power.* Radio-Alger, Algerian Radio-Broadcasting, lost their sovereignty.

Gone were the days when mechanically switching on the radio amounted to an invitation to the enemy. For the Algerian the radio, as a technique, became transformed. The radio set was no longer directly and solely tuned in on the occupier. To the right and to the left of Radio-Alger's broadcasting band, on different and numerous wave-lengths, innumerable stations could be tuned in to, among which it was possible to distinguish the friends, the enemies' accomplices, and the neutrals. Under these conditions, having a receiver was neither making oneself available to the enemy, nor giving him a voice, nor yielding on a point of principle. On the contrary, on the strict level of news, it was showing the desire to keep one's distance, to hear other voices, to take in other prospects. It was in the course of the struggle for liberation and thanks to the creation of a *Voice of Fighting Algeria* that the Algerian experienced and concretely discovered the existence of voices other than the voice of the dominator which formerly had been immeasurably amplified because of his own silence.

The old monologue of the colonial situation, already shaken by the existence of the struggle, disappeared completely by 1956. *The Voice of Fighting Algeria* and all the voices picked up by the receiver now revealed to the Algerian the tenuous, very relative character, in short, the imposture of the French voice presented until now as the only one. The occupier's voice was stripped of its authority.

The nation's *speech,* the nation's spoken *words* shape the world while at the same time renewing it.

Before 1954, native society as a whole rejected the radio, turned a deaf ear to the technical development of methods of news dissemination. There was a non-receptive attitude before this import brought in by the occupier. In the colonial situation, the radio did not satisfy any need of the Algerian people.[11] On the contrary, the radio was considered, as we have seen, a means used by the enemy to quietly carry on his work of depersonalization of the native.

The national struggle and the creation of *Free Radio Algeria* have produced a fundamental change in the people. The radio has appeared in a massive way at once and not in progressive stages. What we have witnessed is a radical transformation of the means of perception, of the very world of perception. Of Algeria it is true to say that there never was, with respect to the radio, a pattern of listening habits, of audience reaction. Insofar as mental processes are concerned, the technique had virtually to be invented. *The Voice of Algeria,* created out of nothing, brought the nation to life and endowed every citizen with a new status, *telling him so explicitly.*

After 1957, the French troops in operation formed the habit of confiscating all the radios in the course of a raid. At the same time listening in on a certain number of broadcasts was prohibited. Today things have progressed. *The Voice of Fighting Algeria* has multiplied. From Tunis, from Damascus, from Cairo, from Rabat, programs are broadcast to the people. The programs are organized by Algerians. The French services no longer try to jam these powerful and numerous broadcasts. The Algerian has the opportunity every day of listening to five or six different broadcasts in Arabic or in French, by means of which he can follow the victorious development of the Revolution step by step. As far as news is concerned, the word of the occupier has been seen to suffer a progressive devaluation. After having imposed the national voice upon that of the dominator, the radio welcomes broadcasts from all the corners of the world.

[11] In this connection may be mentioned the attitude of the French authorities in present-day Algeria. As we know, television was introduced into Algeria several years ago. Until recently, a simultaneous bilingual commentary accompanied the broadcasts. Some time ago, the Arabic commentary ceased. This fact once again confirms the aptness of the formula applied to Radio-Alger: "Frenchmen speaking to Frenchmen."

The "Week of Solidarity with Algeria," organized by the Chinese people, or the resolutions of the Congress of African Peoples on the Algerian war, link the *fellah* to an immense tyranny-destroying wave.

Incorporated under these conditions into the life of the nation, the radio will have an exceptional importance in the country's building phase. After the war a disparity between the people and what is intended to speak for them will no longer be possible. The revolutionary instruction on the struggle for liberation must normally be replaced by a revolutionary instruction on the building of the nation. The fruitful use that can be made of the radio can well be imagined. Algeria has enjoyed a unique experience. For several years, the radio will have been for many, one of the means of saying "no" to the occupation and of believing in the liberation. The identification of the voice of the Revolution with the fundamental truth of the nation has opened limitless horizons.

3

The Algerian Family

We have seen the transformation of the Algerian woman taking place through her revolutionary commitment and her instrumentalization of the veil. It will readily be understood that this radical change could not occur without having profound repercussions on the other components of Algerian family life.

The struggle for national liberation and the more and more total character of the repression have inflicted grave traumatisms upon the family group: a father taken into custody in the street in the company of his children, stripped along with them, tortured before their eyes; the sharply experienced brotherhood of men with bare, bruised, bloody shoulders; a husband arrested, dragged away, imprisoned. The women are then left to find ways of keeping the children from starving to death. We shall come back to this special and very important aspect of the Algerian conflict. We would like here to trace the evolution of the Algerian family, its transformation, the great modifications it has undergone because of and in the course of the war for liberation.

The most important point of this modification, it seems to us, is that the family, from being homogeneous and virtually monolithic, has broken up into separate elements. Each member of this family has gained in individuality what it has lost in its belonging to a world of more or less confused values. Individual persons have found themselves facing new choices, new decisions. The customary and highly structured patterns of behavior that were the crystallization of traditional ideas suddenly proved ineffective and were abandoned. Tradition, in fact, is not solely a combination of automatic gestures and archaic beliefs. At the most elementary level, there are values, and the need for justification. The father questioned by the child explains, comments, legitimizes.

It is important to show that the colonized father at the time of the fight for liberation gave his children the impression of being undecided, of avoiding the taking of sides, even of adopting an evasive and irresponsible attitude. Such an experience, which is traumatic for a child when its points of reference are confined to the family circle, now loses its harmfulness. This experience, in fact, was occurring on a national scale and was part and parcel of the great upheaval incidental to the creation of a new world which was felt throughout the territory.

Before 1954, the existence of nationalist parties had already introduced changes into the native private life. The nationalist parties, the parliamentary political action, the spreading of slogans advocating splitting off from France, had already given rise to certain contradictions within the family. These developments invited the inert resistance of the colonized society to turn into action. For the tense immobility of the dominated society, the nationalist parties tried to substitute awareness, movement, creation. The people, as a whole, agreed with these parties, but they had a sharp memory of the legendary ferocity of the French military and police. Witnesses of the colonial invasion, still alive 30 or 40 years ago, had often related to them episodes of the conquest. In many regions of Algeria the accounts of massacres and the burning of villages were still vividly remembered. The conqueror had settled in such numbers, he had created so many centers of colonization, that a certain passivity encouraged by the colonial domination made itself evident and gradually took on a tinge of despair. Before 1954, the son who adopted a nationalist position never did so, really, against his father's wishes, but his activity as a militant in any case never in any respect modified his filial behavior within the framework of the Algerian family. The relations based on the absolute respect due to the father and on the principle that the truth is first of all the unchallengeable property of the elders were not encroached upon. Modesty, shame, the fear of looking at the father, of speaking aloud in his presence, remained intact, even in the case of the nationalist militant. The absence of actual revolutionary action kept the personality in its customary channels.

For a long time, political action in a colonized country is a legal action that is carried on within the parliamentary framework. After a certain period, when official and peaceful channels are exhausted, the militant hardens his position. The political party passes over to direct action, and the problems that the son faces are problems of life or death for the country. In a parallel way, his attitude toward his father and the other members of the family frees itself of everything that proves unnecessary and detrimental to the revolutionary situation. The person is born, assumes his autonomy, and becomes the creator of his own values. The old stultifying attachment to the father melts in the sun of the Revolution. In Algeria, after Sétif and the different combats waged by the nationalist parties during the postwar period, positions sharpened and the people's political maturity markedly progressed.

On November 1, 1954, the Revolution reopened all the problems: those of colonialism, but also those of the colonized society. *The colonized society perceived that in order to succeed in the gigantic undertaking into which it had flung itself, in order to defeat colonialism and in order to build the Algerian nation, it would have to make a vast effort of self-preparation, strain all its joints, renew its blood and its soul.* In the course of the multiple episodes of the war, the people came to realize that if they wished to bring a new world to birth they would have to create a new Algerian society from top to bottom. In order to fulfill his aspirations, the Algerian must adapt himself at an exceptional pace to this new situation. The truth, for once, eluded its traditional trustees and placed itself within reach of any seeker. The group, which formerly looked to the father to determine its values, now had to seek these each for himself, as circumstances dictated.

Every Algerian faced with the new system of values introduced by the Revolution is compelled to define himself, to take a position, to choose.

The Son and the Father

At the time when the people were called upon to adopt radical forms of struggle, the Algerian family was still highly structured. But on the level of national consciousness, the father lagged far behind the son. A new world had come into being long before, which the parents knew nothing about, and which was developing with exceptional rapidity. In a confused way, it is true, the father had caught in passing a few snatches of phrases, a few sharp-edged meanings, but never came to the decision to fight the occupant, weapons in hand. Yet there was not an Algerian who had not faced the challenge of the oppression and wondered what was to be done. Every Algerian, at least at one time in his life, in the course of a meeting, or simply a discussion, had wished for the defeat of colonialism. At the market, in a café, on a pilgrimage, in the course of the traditional holidays, there always came a moment when the Algerian plotted against the occupier. But these exchanges were like the desperate lamentations of all the humiliated of all the countries in the world. The deep hold taken by colonial society, its frenzy to transform itself into a necessity, the wretchedness on which it was built, gave to life that familiar tinge of resignation that specialists in underdeveloped countries describe under the heading of *fatalism*.

And it was in these inauspicious circumstances that the first salvos of November 1954 burst forth. Before the Revolution, which abruptly split the world in two, the father found himself disarmed and a little anxious. This anxiety was transformed into confusion in the presence of the son, who would become absorbed and tense. Thus a whole atmosphere was created, tragic, unrelieved, heightened by the ever-present French police whose vigilance could be sensed, and the whole European city that pointed its hatred, like a gun, at the Algerian quarter. Parents very often react according to a uniform pattern. The kind of observations that had been made before 1954 reappeared, and the familiar prudent advice was brought out. But this was also accompanied by defeatist remarks: "Don't make a move; the French are too strong; you'll never succeed." The son would dodge discussion, avoid answering, would try not to bring out into the open a clash between the new world he was building and the father's universe of infinite waiting and resignation. Sometimes the father would require that the son remain quiet, give up the struggle, come back to the family and take care of his own. Bachelors were told that they should think about marriage, and married men were reminded of their duties. Disagreement became overt. The young Algerian would feel called upon to defend his position, to justify his line of behavior before his father. He would firmly condemn and reject the father's counsels of prudence. *But he would not reject and ban the father*. What he would try to do, on the contrary, would be to convert the family. The militant would replace the son and undertake to indoctrinate the father. But it would not be the son's words that would convince him. It would be, more than anything, the dimensions of the people's commitment, the information received as to the repression. The old paternal assurance, already shaken, would collapse once and for all. The father no longer knew how to keep his balance. He would then discover that the only way to do it was to join his son. It was during this period that the father buried the old values and decided to follow along on the new path. Jacques Lanzmann, in his last book, *Viva Castro,* finds the same phenomenon in Cuban society during the Castro Revolution:

"From as early as we can remember, in our country, and this was a matter of profound belief and acceptance, the father owed it to himself to teach, to transmit his experience to his son. That experience, señor, was the thread that sewed together the members of the same family. In essential matters, the son always shared his father's views. You no doubt know the Cuban proverb, 'Like father, like son?' "

"Naturally," I said.

"Accordingly, the father and the son were as one, until the day when a man who had taken refuge in the mountains and who was himself very young, took our sons from us. That man is a kind of Christ, I tell you! What is a father, compared to a Christ? Nothing, señor. So we fathers asked ourselves why our sons had left us. We tried to find in our poor heads the reason for such a separation and we thought, señor, that our experience of almost a hundred years was wrong. It was no good, our experience, it was just a life of every day that we passed on, somehow, without too much thinking about it, from father to son, for generations. One single man was sufficient, a man who had nothing to offer but idealism and purity. It was better than our experience, our money, our jobs, our relations."[1]

This conversion of the father, however, did not totally eliminate traditional patterns of behavior. It was difficult for the father to stifle both his desire to re-establish his collapsed sovereignty and his obsession with the frightful consequences of this open war. Thus new forms of paternal opposition, veiled manifestations of paternal authority, came to light. When, for example, a young Algerian would decide to join the maquis, the father would no longer formally forbid it. He would appeal, rather, to the young man's sense of discipline as a militant, and would ask if he were leaving in response to a mobilization call or if he were doing so on his own initiative. In the latter case, the father would be the first to remind the militant-son of the principles of discipline: if your chiefs need you, they will call you. Thus in order to oppose an act—going into the maquis—which, after 1956, endangered the lives of other members of the family who remained at home, the father had no other resources than to recognize the new values and to invoke other authorities.

At no time do we find a really painful clash. The father stood back before the new world and followed in his son's footsteps. It was the young Algerian who swept the family into the vast national liberation movement. Sometimes, however, the situation was more difficult. The father might be a notorious collab-

[1] J. Lanzmann, *Viva Castro,* p. 114.

orationist with the colonialist administration. In the very exercise of his profession, this man would find himself cornered into making an irrevocable choice: being a *caïd* (a police agent), a *bachagha* (an official holding office by virtue of a rigged election), he would be both rejected and condemned by the new Algeria that his son embodied. Very often he would resign. However, it might happen that the contamination was such that he was no longer able to free himself from the colonialist embrace. The long succession of compromises was so imposing that there could be no turning back. Several Algerian families have experienced those atrocious tragedies in which the son, present at a meeting that had to decide the fate of his father who was a traitor to his fatherland, had no other choice but to support the majority and accept the most irrevocable judgments. At other times the son would be called upon in the Committee to set the amount of money that was to be demanded of his parents as their contribution to the Revolution, and one can readily imagine the paradox of the situation of a father complaining to his son as he would to an associate about the enormous sum exacted by the leaders. This defeat of the father by the new forces that were emerging could not fail to modify the relations that had formerly prevailed in Algerian society.

The Daughter and the Father

In the Algerian family, the girl is always one notch behind the boy. As in all societies in which work on the land represents the main source of the means of subsistence, the male, who is the privileged producer, enjoys an almost lordly status. The birth of a boy in a family is greeted with greater enthusiasm than that of a girl. The father sees in him a future working partner, a successor to the family plot and after his death a guardian for the mother and the sisters. The young girl, without being humiliated or neglected, cannot help being aware of the fuss made over her brother.

The girl has no opportunity, all things considered, to develop her personality or to take any initiative. She takes her place in the vast network of domestic traditions of Algerian society. The woman's life in the home, made up of centuries-old customs, allows no innovation. Illiteracy, poverty, the status of an oppressed people, maintain and strengthen the specific features of the colonized universe, to the point of changing their entire nature. The girl adopts automatically the behavior and the values of Algerian feminine society. From her mother she learns the higher value of the man. The woman in an underdeveloped society, and particularly in Algeria, is always a minor, and the man—brother, uncle or husband—represents first of all a guardian. The young girl learns to avoid discussions with the man, not to "aggravate the man." The facility with which divorce is obtained in Algerian society imposes upon the woman the weight of an almost obsessional fear of being sent back to her family. The boy, for his part, adopts the father's attitude.

Rather quickly, in the family, the young girl avoids appearing before the father. When the woman replaces the girl at the time of puberty, there is a kind of tacit agreement to the effect that the father shall never be alone with his daughter. Everything is organized so as to keep the father in ignorance of the fact that his daughter has reached puberty. The father will say that it does not concern him, but in reality he wants to put off facing the girl's new situation. This necessity that the father feels not to be exposed to the new woman who has come into the home, leads the family to contemplate the girl's marriage. Early marriage in Algeria is not motivated by the desire to reduce the number of mouths to feed, but quite literally by the wish not to acquire a new woman without status, a childwoman, in the house. The girl who comes to womanhood must marry and have children. To have a girl who has reached puberty in the house is an extremely difficult problem for a family. The girl at puberty is available for marriage, which explains the rigor with which she is kept in the home, protected, and watched over. This also explains the ease with which she is married off.

Under these conditions it will readily be understood that a girl wanting to choose her own husband or refusing the man proposed to her by her family would encounter considerable opposition. The girl who senses her parents' anxiety and who experiences the precariousness of her new situation as a child-woman looks upon marriage as a liberation, as a deliverance, as achieving finally her balance. The life of an Algerian woman does not develop according to the three periods known in the West—childhood, puberty, and marriage. The Algerian girl knows only two stages—childhood-puberty, and marriage. The girl who reaches puberty in Algeria and does not marry prolongs an abnormal situation. It must never be forgotten that the illiteracy and the unemployment that prevail in Algeria leave the girl no other solution. In a *douar,* the unmarried woman—and a girl becomes a woman at sixteen—must marry. Considered a minor indefinitely, the woman owes it to herself to find a husband as soon as possible, and the father is haunted by the fear of dying and abandoning his daughter without support and therefore unable to survive.

All these restrictions were to be knocked over and challenged by the national liberation struggle. The unveiled Algerian woman, who assumed an increasingly important place in revolutionary action, developed her personality, discovered the exalting realm of responsibility. The freedom of the Algerian people from then on became identified with woman's liberation, with her entry into history. This woman who, in the avenues of Algiers or of Constantine, would carry the grenades or the submachine-gun chargers, this woman who tomorrow would be outraged, violated, tortured, could not put herself back into her former state of mind and relive her behavior of the past; this woman who was writing the heroic pages of Algerian history was, in so doing, bursting the bounds of the narrow world in which she had lived without responsibility, and was at the same time participating in the destruction of colonialism and in the birth of a new woman.

The women in Algeria, from 1955, began to have models. In Algerian society stories were told of women who in ever greater number suffered death and imprisonment in order that an independent Algeria might be born. It was these militant women who constituted the points of reference around which the imagination of Algerian feminine society was to be stirred to the boiling point. The woman-for-marriage progressively disappeared, and gave way to the woman-for-action. The young girl was replaced by the militant, the woman by the *sister*.

The female cells of the F.L.N. received mass memberships. The impatience of these new recruits was so great that it often endangered the traditions of complete secrecy. The leaders had to restrain the exceptional enthusiasm and radicalism that are always characteristic of any youth engaged in building a new world. As soon as they were enrolled, these women would ask to be given the most dangerous assignments. Only progressively did the political training that was given them lead them away from contemplating the struggle in an explosive form. The Algerian girl learned to contain her impatience and to show unexpected virtues of calm, composure and firmness.

It would happen that a girl would be sought after by the police or that several members of the group she belonged to would be arrested. The necessity to vanish, to make her getaway, would become urgent. The militant would first leave her family and take refuge with friends. But soon orders would come from the network leadership to join the nearest maquis. After all the previous shocks—the daughter relinquishing the veil, putting on makeup, going out at all hours heaven knew where, etc.—the parents no longer dared protest. The father himself no longer had any choice. His old fear of dishonor had become altogether absurd in the light of the immense tragedy being experienced by the people. But apart from this, the national authority that had decided that the girl should leave for the maquis would have no patience with such reticence on the father's part. Challenging the morality of a patriot had been ruled out long ago. Moreover, there was the overriding consideration of the combat—hard, intense, implacable. There was no time to lose. So the girl would go up into the maquis, alone with men. For months and months, the parents would be without news of a girl of eighteen who would sleep in the forests or in the grottoes, who would roam the *djebel* dressed as a man, with a gun in her hands.

The father's attitude toward the girls remaining at home or toward any other woman met in the street inevitably underwent a radical change. And the girl who had not gone into the maquis, who was not actively engaged, became aware of the important role played by women in the revolutionary struggle. The men's words were no longer law. The women were no longer silent. Algerian society in the fight for liberation, in the sacrifices that it was willing to make in order to liberate itself from colonialism, renewed itself and developed new values governing sexual relations. The woman ceased to be a complement for man. *She literally forged a new place for herself by her sheer strength.*

Sometimes the girl would come down from the mountain, carrying a new identity card. She would then have the opportunity of telling the father and the mother what prodigious actions were taking place every day in the *djebel.* She would show photographs. She would speak of her chiefs, of her *brothers,* of the population, the wounded, the French prisoners. She would look at the father, she would sit facing the father, would speak to him and not be embarrassed. And the father would not turn his face away; he would not feel shame. On the contrary, he would feel a real joy at seeing his daughter again, at seeing her new personality radiating through the house; he would not be displeased to hear his daughter speaking out and it would absolutely not occur to him to remind her that a woman should be silent. For the three days of her leave, the father would feel no need to question his daughter as to her moral behavior in the maquis. This silence did not betray a lack of interest or a resignation with respect to yesterday's demand of virginity. It was rather because the father could gauge the immense step taken by society, and these questions that were still present to his mind revealed themselves to be inappropriate and irrelevant. The Algerian girl who was emerging into the agitated arena of history was inviting her father to undergo a kind of mutation, to wrench himself free of himself. To ask of a woman who was daily risking her life whether she was "serious" became grotesque and absurd. The militant girl, in adopting new patterns of conduct, could not be judged by traditional standards. Old values, sterile and infantile phobias disappeared.

The Brothers

In Algeria, the eldest brother is the father's designated successor. The other members of the family very quickly adopt a respectful and deferential attitude toward him. A certain number of things are not done in the eldest brother's presence. One is careful not to be with him in the same group of youngsters where more or less frivolous jokes are likely to be heard. The attitude of the younger brother toward his big brother is comparable to that of the son toward the father. The disruption that we have seen in the relations of father and son is to be found here too, but is particularly accentuated. Brothers may in fact be active in the same cell and when the network is discovered may join the maquis. They fight in the same unit, suffer together from hunger and at times from shortage of ammunition. The measured and ritual relations of the pre-war period give way to totally new relations. The two brothers are integrated in a specific action and obey a single authority.[2]

The old relationship confined within the closed circuit of the family underwent radical changes. It would even happen that the younger son would be the group leader. And the traditional respect for the big brother did not inhibit the political or military chief. Invested with a power within the framework of the Revolution, the *brother* was led to go beyond the stereotyped, automatic ways of behavior. The *man* who seemed to disappear behind the *brother* now came to the fore. The older brother was no longer necessarily right, and each one now defined his own values.

[2] In the period before the Revolution, brothers working in the same plant would ask the foreman to be assigned to different jobs. In a hospital, too, two brothers who were nurses would go out of their way to be assigned to different wards.

The Couple

The relations of wife and husband have likewise become modified in the course of the war of liberation. Whereas everyone in the house formerly had well-defined functions, the intensity of the struggle was to impose unanticipated types of behavior.

Let us take the case of Mustapha. Mustapha has just come home. A little while ago, with another *fidaï,* he has thrown several grenades into the premises of the Judicial Police where patriots are being tortured night and day. He does not feel like talking. He lies down and shuts his eyes. His wife has seen him come in but has noticed nothing. An hour later, the news floods the district: two patriots have successfully carried out a spectacular coup. In the alleyway and in the court, the casualties of the adversary are estimated. The angry patrols that are already pouring into the streets are irrefutable proof that our people have dealt the colonists a hard blow. The woman comes back into the room, and seeing her husband slumbering, impervious to what has happened, gives vent to her contempt: "You wouldn't be up to doing a thing like that! It's easier to sleep and eat." And she goes on to mention a neighbor who has been thrown into prison, another executed by the enemy, and finally the cousin who has sent pictures from the maquis. Treated as a coward by his wife, Mustapha remains silent, doubly pleased by his wife's healthy anger and by the success of his assignment.

This example, a fairly typical occurrence in 1956, is of considerable interest. In relations between men in Algeria, accusing a man of cowardice is an insult for which reparation can be made only in blood. It is not permitted to cast doubt on a man's courage or on his virility; no one can accept that. And when the accuser is a woman, things become absolutely intolerable.

The struggle for liberation raised woman to such a level of inner renewal that she is even able to call her husband a coward. Rather frequently, by allusions or explicitly, the Algerian woman would upbraid her husband for his inactivity, his refusal to commit himself, his lack of militancy. This was the period when young girls among themselves would vow never to let themselves be married to a man who did not belong to the F.L.N. The Algerian woman, in throwing caution to the winds, at the same time divests herself of the instinct to protect her home. Reproaching one's husband for not participating in a combat known to be deadly is a paradoxical kind of behavior, to say the least. But the women no longer consider the man's conditions as they did before. The man's job is patriotic activity and no one can affirm his virility if he is not a part of the fighting nation.

Sometimes, however, the woman was not uninformed as to her husband's activity. A militant of long standing, the husband would frequently vanish, and sometimes she would find a revolver under his pillow. As the searches multiplied, the woman demanded of her husband that he keep her informed. She would insist on being given certain names and addresses of militants to warn in case the husband should be arrested. It was on the grounds of effectiveness that she persuaded her husband to allow her to become involved in action. She would invoke, for example, the case of a militant who, under torture, had given names and thereby caused the destruction of a whole network, and she would warn her husband against wanting to be "the only one in the know," out of a false pride concealing itself behind the mask of secrecy. Little by little, resistances disappeared and the united militant couple, participating in the birth of the nation, became the rule in Algeria.

Sometimes the husband, who had been away in the maquis for several months, would come back on leave. Overcome by the enveloping warmth of the home, he would confide to his wife his desire not to go back "up there." The wife who had resumed, with an intensity that can be imagined, her dimension as a woman, would share with her husband the need to prolong and not interrupt those completely "lived" hours that seemed to escape time. And as always, in such cases, the frenzy with which every moment was savored was conditioned by the ever possible eventuality of a death that might, any day, separate them forever. Yet it would be the woman who would ask her husband to banish such an idea from his mind. "What will you say to the people of the village when they ask you questions? You promised to come back once independence had been won; you swore to bring back freedom. How can you consider resuming a normal life when all the men are up there or in prison?"

Often the childless woman, witnessing the mass involvement of the nation, seeing the young girls of the village leaving one after another, would decide to join her husband. She would of course not see him often, but in periods of relative calm the couple could come together. It was not unusual for the woman arriving in the maquis to learn of the death of her husband. Often she would return to the village to her parents' home, but sometimes the shock would make her decide to stay with the fighters and take part in the struggle for liberation. The woman's presence in the maquis would disturb the husband much less than her militant activity in the centers. The woman who would set out on a mission three hundred kilometers from her domicile, who would sleep wherever she could, among unknown companions, inevitably created a certain number of problems for the husband. They were never formulated, to be sure, but no revolution can, with finality and without repercussions, make a clean sweep of well-nigh instinctive modes of behavior. "You can't imagine what it's like to hear someone asking for your wife on the telephone. You call your wife, you hand her the receiver, and you hear yourself being invited to leave the room; then your wife goes off and sometimes comes back four hours or four days later. You are given no explanation, but you cannot be unaware of the action in which she is involved, since you yourself were the one who mobilized her. You yourself were the one who taught her the strict rules of absolute secrecy."

The Algerian couple has become considerably more closely knit in the course of this Revolution. The sometimes fragile bonds, marked by the precarious nature of the present, of what could be rejected from one moment to the next, were strengthened, or at least changed character. What could formerly be defined as mere cohabitation today includes a multiplicity of points of communication. First and foremost is the fact of incurring dangers together, of turning over in the same bed, each on his own side, each with his fragment of a secret. It is also the consciousness of collaborating in the immense work of destroying the world of oppression. The couple is no longer shut in upon itself. It no longer finds its end in itself. It is no longer the result of the natural instinct of perpetuation of the species, nor the institutionalized means of satisfying one's sexuality. The couple becomes the basic cell of the commonwealth, the fertile nucleus of the nation. The Algerian couple, in becoming a link in the revolutionary organization, is transformed into a unit of existence. *The mingling of fighting experience with conjugal life deepens the relations between husband and wife and cements their union. There is a simultaneous and effervescent emergence of the citizen, the patriot, and the modern spouse.* The Algerian couple rids itself of its traditional weaknesses at the same time that the solidarity of the people becomes a part of history. This couple is no longer an accident but something rediscovered, willed, built. It is, as we can see, the very foundation of the sexual encounter that we are concerned with here.

Marriage and Divorce

In Algeria marriage is generally decided by the families. It is almost always at the wedding that the husband sees his wife's face for the first time. The social and economic reasons for this tradition are sufficiently well known and need not be explained here. Marriage in the underdeveloped countries is not an individual contract, but a contract between clan and clan, tribe and tribe, family and family.

With the Revolution, things were gradually to change. The presence of women in the maquis, the contact between unmarried men and women, created unexpected problems for the local F.L.N. leaders. Men would go to their superior officer and ask to marry such and such a nurse. The F.L.N. officer would hesitate for a long time. No one can give a girl away in marriage, except her father, and in the father's absence, her uncle or her brother. The officer did not feel he had a right to entertain the *moudjahid's* request and sometimes found himself obliged to separate the two lovers. But love is an incontrovertible fact which must be reckoned with, and the leadership of the Revolution gave instructions that marriages could be contracted before a mayor or registry official.

Registry offices were opened. Marriages, births, and deaths could then be registered. Marriage in the maquis ceased to be an arrangement between families. All unions were voluntary. The future wife and husband had had time to know each other, to esteem, to love each other. Even the case of love at first sight had been anticipated by the directives. Whenever an application for marriage is presented, the instructions read, it is well to postpone any decision for three months. When the father learned of the marriage of his daughter in the maquis, the act would not be contested or condemned. On the contrary, pictures would be asked for, and the babies born in the maquis would be sent to the grandparents who would care for these children of the Revolution as they deserved.

Such innovations could not fail to have repercussions on the traditional modes of marriage that continued to be practiced in the rest of the country. Algerian women began at first to demand guarantees of the future husband's patriotism. They would require that the young men who were being proposed to them be members of the F.L.N. The father's unchallengeable and massive authority let itself be shaken by this new requirement. Before the Revolution, a girl who had been asked for as a wife would leave the family circle for several days and take refuge with relatives. This is explained by the shame felt by the girl at being the object of a sexual pursuit. It was also usual for the young bride to avoid appearing before her father for one or two months after the consummation of the marriage. These modest, infantile patterns of behavior disappeared with the Revolution and today the majority of young married women have themselves been present at the signature of their contract and have naturally been consulted as to their intended. Marriage in Algeria underwent this radical transformation in the very heart of the combat waged by the *Moudjahidines* and the *Moudjahidates.*

Under these conditions, divorce, the separation of husband and wife, was bound to undergo change. The husband's repudiation of his wife that could be immediately proclaimed at any time and that reflected the fragility of the conjugal bond is no longer automatically legalized. The husband must explain his reasons for wanting a divorce. There are attempts at reconciliation. In any case, the final decision rests with the local officer. The family emerges strengthened from this ordeal in which colonialism has resorted to every means to break the people's will. In the midst of the gravest dangers the Algerian adopts modern forms of existence and confers on the human person his maximum independence.

Feminine Society

The women who participate in the war and who marry in the maquis have initiated within Algerian feminine society radical changes in certain patterns of behavior. A one-sided interpretation of the main changes observed must, however, be avoided. The war waged by French colonialism obliges the Algerian people to be constantly and wholly engaged in the battle. Confronted by an adversary who has sworn to keep Algeria, even without the Algerians, it is difficult to remain oneself, to maintain preferences or values intact. Feminine society undergoes change both through an organic solidarity with the Revolution, and more especially because the adversary cuts into the Algerian flesh with unheard-of violence.

The women, accustomed to going to the village cemetery or to visiting a local sanctuary on Fridays, interrupt this activity among others when they are regrouped along with tens of thousands of other families.[3]

In the camp they immediately organize themselves in F.L.N. cells. They meet women from other regions, exchange their experiences of the repression—but also their experiences from before the Revolution, their hopes. The regrouped Algerian woman, cut off from her husband who has remained with the combatants, takes care of the old and the orphans, learns to read and to sew and often, in a group of several companions, leaves the camp and joins the Army of National Liberation.

With these considerable shifts in population, the whole social panorama and the perceptual framework are disturbed and restructured. A *mechta* evacuated is not a *mechta* that has migrated.[4] The chain of events of the operation must be patiently followed: bombardments of the region, multiple raids, able-bodied men taking to the mountains, the dead quickly buried, the hostages taken away by the French, certain members of the *mechta* taking refuge in a neighboring town with relatives or friends.

The regrouped *mechta* is a broken, destroyed *mechta*. It is merely a group of men, women and children. Under these conditions, no gesture is kept intact. No previous rhythm is to be found unaltered. Caught in the meshes of the barbed wires, the members of regrouped Algerian families neither eat nor sleep as they did before. This can be seen, for example, on the occasion of a death. The lamentations, the wails, the grief-stricken faces, and the contortions of the body have today practically disappeared. The classic mourning tears are hardly any longer to be found in Algeria. All this began in 1955 when the French troops, for the fun of it, or in the course of a repression, would overrun a locality and machinegun five or ten men. These collective deaths, without warning, without a previous illness

[3] The French colonialist forces, as we know, have put more than a million Algerians behind barbed wires. These are the notorious "regrouping centers" in which, as the French authorities themselves admit, disease and mortality run to abnormally high figures.

[4] *mechta*—a hamlet. (Translator's note)

that had been treated and fought, abandoned in the ditch on the edge of the road, cannot set into motion emotional mechanisms that are homogeneous to a society. Lamentations and grief-stricken faces are part of a patterned, stable world. One does not weep, one does not do as before when one is faced with multiple murders. One grits one's teeth and one prays in silence. One further step, and it is cries of joy that salute the death of a *moudjahid* who has fallen on the field of honor. It must not be believed, however, that the traditional ceremonies are repeated in the case of natural deaths, resulting from illnesses or accidents. Even then, it seems virtually impossible to revive the habitual techniques of despair. The war has dislocated Algerian society to such a point that any death is conceived of as a direct or indirect consequence of colonialist repression. Today there is not a dead person in Algeria who is not the victim of French colonialism. It is impossible for an Algerian civilian to remain untouched by the war of colonial reconquest. More than this, there is not a death of an Algerian outside of Algeria which is not attributed to French colonialism. The Algerian people have thus decided that, until independence, French colonialism will be innocent of none of the wounds inflicted upon its body and its consciousness.

Algeria Dispersed

The tactic adopted by French colonialism since the beginning of the Revolution has had the result of separating the people from each other, of fragmenting them, with the sole objective of making any cohesion impossible. This effort was at first concentrated on the men, who were interned by tens of thousands. It is well known that in 1955-56, the number of internment centers multiplied rapidly over the national territory. Lodi, Paul Cazelles, Berrouaghia have held fathers and husbands captive for years. The Algerian woman, suddenly deprived of a husband, is obliged to find a means of feeding her children. She finds herself having to go from place to place, to run her errands, to live without the man's protection. Sometimes she will go and visit her husband interned a hundred or two hundred kilometers from his home. When the men are not interned, they are to be found in the maquis, and the mothers who receive the family allowances distributed by the Liberation Front are left all alone to raise the children. In the cities the prison gates close on an imposing number of Algerian men, and in order to flee the regroupment camps, in order to escape the repeated bombardments of French planes, tens of thousands of families have taken refuge in Tunisia and in Morocco.

The multiple murders of Algerian men and women by French colonialism have particularly attracted the world's attention and have given rise to the wave of protests that we have seen. But we must try to look more closely at the reality of Algeria. We must not simply fly over it. We must, on the contrary, walk step by step along the great wound inflicted on the Algerian soil and on the Algerian people. We must question the Algerian earth meter by meter, and measure the fragmentation of the Algerian family, the degree to which it finds itself scattered. A woman led away by soldiers who comes back a week later—it is unnecessary to question her to understand that she has been violated dozens of times. A husband taken away by the enemy who comes back with his body covered with contusions, more dead than alive, his mind stunned. Children scattered to the winds, innumerable orphans who roam about, haggard and famished. When a man welcomes his wife who has spent two weeks in a French camp and he says hello to her and asks her if she is hungry, and he avoids looking at her and bows his head—when such things are a daily occurrence, it is not possible to imagine that the Algerian family can have remained intact and that hatred of colonialism has not swelled immeasurably. French colonialism since 1954 has wanted nothing other than to break the will of the people, to destroy its resistance, to liquidate its hopes. For five years it has avoided no extremist tactic, whether of terror or of torture. In stirring up these men and women, colonialism has regrouped them beneath a single sign. Equally victims of the same tyranny, simultaneously identifying a single enemy, this physically dispersed people is realizing its unity and founding in suffering a spiritual community which constitutes the most solid bastion of the Algerian Revolution.

4

Medicine and Colonialism

The Algerian Example

Introduced into Algeria at the same time as racialism and humiliation, Western medical science, being part of the oppressive system, has always provoked in the native an ambivalent attitude. This ambivalence is in fact to be found in connection with all of the occupier's modes of presence. With medicine we come to one of the most tragic features of the colonial situation.

In all objectivity and in all humanity, it is a good thing that a technically advanced country benefits from its knowledge and the discoveries of its scientists. When the discipline considered concerns man's health, when its very principle is to ease pain, it is clear that no negative reaction can be justified. But the colonial situation is precisely such that it drives the colonized to appraise all the colonizer's contributions in a pejorative and absolute way. The colonized perceives the doctor, the engineer, the schoolteacher, the policeman, the rural constable, through the haze of an almost organic confusion. The compulsory visit by the doctor to the *douar* is preceded by the assembling of the population through the agency of the police authorities. The doctor who arrives in this atmosphere of general constraint is never a native doctor but always a doctor belonging to the dominant society and very often to the army.

The statistics on sanitary improvements are not interpreted by the native as progress in the fight against illness, in general, but as fresh proof of the extension of the occupier's hold on the country. When the French authorities show visitors through the Tizi-Ouzou sanitorium or the operating units of the Mustapha hospital in Algiers, this has for the native just one meaning: "This is what we have done for the people of this country; this country owes us everything; were it not for us, there would be no country." There is a real mental reservation on the part of the native; it is difficult for him to be objective, to separate the wheat from the chaff.

There are of course exceptions. In certain periods of calm, in certain free confrontations, the colonized individual frankly recognizes what is positive in the dominator's action. But this good faith is immediately taken advantage of by the occupier and transformed into a justification of the occupation. When the native, after a major effort in the direction of truth, because he assumes that his defenses have been surmounted, says, "That is good. I tell you so because I think so," the colonizer perverts his meaning and translates, "Don't leave, for what would we do without you?"

Thus, on the level of the whole colonized society, we always discover this reluctance to qualify opposition to the colonialist, for it so happens that every qualification is perceived by the occupier as an invitation to perpetuate the oppression, as a confession of congenital impotence. The colonized people as a whole, when faced with certain happenings, will react in a harsh, undifferentiated, categorical way before the dominant group's activity. It is not unusual to hear such extreme observations as this: "Nobody asked you for anything; who invited you to come? Take your hospitals and your port facilities and go home."

The fact is that the colonization, having been built on military conquest and the police system, sought a justification for its existence and the legitimization of its persistence in its works.

Reduced, in the name of truth and reason, to saying "yes" to certain innovations of the occupier, the colonized perceived that he thus became the prisoner of the entire system, and that the French medical service in Algeria could not be separated from French colonialism in Algeria. Then, as he could not cut himself off from his people, who aspired to a national existence on their own soil, he rejected doctors, schoolteachers, engineers, parachutists, all in one lump.

In a non-colonial society, the attitude of a sick man in the presence of a medical practitioner is one of confidence. The patient trusts the doctor; he puts himself in his hands. He yields his body to him. He accepts the fact that pain may be awakened or exacerbated by the physician, for the patient realizes that the intensifying of suffering in the course of examination may pave the way to peace in his body.

At no time, in a non-colonial society, does the patient mistrust his doctor. On the level of technique, of knowledge, it is clear that a certain doubt can filter into the patient's mind, but this may be due to a hesitation on the part of the doctor which modifies the original confidence. This can happen anywhere. But it is obvious that certain circumstances can appreciably change the doctor-patient relationship. The German prisoner who was to be operated on by a French surgeon would very often, just before being given the anaesthetic, beseech the doctor not to kill him. Under the same circumstances, the surgeon might be more than ordinarily anxious to perform the operation successfully because of the other prisoners, because he realized the interpretation that might be given the event if a patient died on the operating table. The French prisoners in the German camps showed a similar concern when they asked the doctors working in the camp infirmary to assist in the operations performed by German surgeons. Literature and the motion pictures have made much of such situations, and after every war the problems they involve are commercially exploited.

In colonial territory such situations are to be found in even greater number. The sudden deaths of Algerians in hospitals, a common occurrence in any establishment caring for the sick and the injured, are interpreted as the effects of a murderous and deliberate decision, as the result of criminal maneuvers on the part of the European doctor. The Algerian's refusal to be hospitalized is always more or less related to that lingering doubt as to the colonial doctor's essential humanity. It needs to be said, too, although it is not the rule, that in certain hospital services experimentation on living patients is practiced to an extent that cannot be considered negligible.[1]

For dozens of years, despite the doctor's exhortations, the Algerian shied away from hospitalization. Even though the specialist might insist that any hesitation would seriously endanger the patient's life, the patient would hang back and refuse to be taken to the hospital. It would always be at the last moment, when hardly any hope remained, that consent was given. Even then, the man who made the decision would make it in opposition to the group; and as the case would be a desperate one, as the decision had been too long delayed, the patient would usually die.

Such experiences would strengthen the group in its original belief in the occupier's fundamentally evil character, even though he was a doctor. And the Algerian who, after considerable effort, had succeeded in overcoming the traditional prejudice to an appreciable extent, who had forced the decision to hospitalize the patient, would suddenly feel infinitely guilty. Inwardly he would promise not to repeat his mistake. The values of the group, momentarily abandoned, would reassert themselves, in an exacerbated and exclusive way.

It would be a serious mistake, and it would in any case make such an attitude incomprehensible, to compare such behavior with that already described as characterizing the poor rural populations of European countries. The colonized who resisted

[1] French soldiers hospitalized in the psychiatric services of the French Army in Algeria have all seen the experimental epileptic fits produced in Algerians and in infantrymen from south of the Sahara, for the purpose of estimating the specific threshold of each of the different races. These men on whom the French doctors practiced these experiments were brought to the hospital on the "scientific pretext" of having to make further examinations.

It was left to the Algerian society alone, to the Algerian people alone, to manifest through combat its determination to put an end to such infamies, among others, on the national soil.

hospitalization did not do so on the basis of the fear of cities, the fear of distance, of no longer being protected by the family, the fear that people would say that the patient had been sent to the hospital to die, that the family had rid itself of a burden. The colonized not only refused to send the patient to the hospital, but he refused to send him to the hospital of the whites, of strangers, of the conqueror.

It is necessary to analyze, patiently and lucidly, each one of the reactions of the colonized, and every time we do not understand, we must tell ourselves that we are at the heart of the drama—that of the impossibility of finding a meeting ground in any colonial situation. For some time it was maintained that the native's reluctance to entrust himself to a European doctor was due to his attachment to his traditional medical techniques or to his dependence on the sorcerers or healers of his group. Such psychological reactions do obviously exist, and they were to be observed, not too many years ago, not only among the masses of generally advanced countries, but also among doctors themselves. Leriche has reported to us the hesitancies or the refusals of certain doctors to adopt the thermometer because they were accustomed to estimating the temperature by taking the pulse. Examples of this kind could be indefinitely multiplied. It is hardly abnormal, therefore, for individuals accustomed to practicing certain customs in the treatment of a given ailment, to adopting certain procedures when confronted with the disorder that illness constitutes, to refuse to abandon these customs and procedures because others are imposed on them, in other words because the new technique takes over completely and does not tolerate the persistence of any shred of tradition.

Here again we hear the same refrain: "If I abandon what I am in the habit of doing when my wife coughs and I authorize the European doctor to give her injections; if I find myself literally insulted and told I am a savage [this happens], because I have made scratches on the forehead of my son who has been complaining of a headache for three days; if I tell this insulter he is right and I admit that I was wrong to make those scratches which custom has taught me to do—if I do all these things I am acting, from a strictly rational point of view, in a positive way. For, as a matter of fact, my son has meningitis and it really has to be treated as a meningitis ought to be treated. But the colonial constellation is such that what should be the brotherly and tender insistence of one who wants only to help me is interpreted as a manifestation of the conqueror's arrogance and desire to humiliate."

It is not possible for the colonized society and the colonizing society to agree to pay tribute, at the same time and in the same place, to a single value. If, against all probability, the colonized society expresses its agreement on any point with the colonizing society, there will at once begin to be talk about successful integration. It is now necessary to enter into the tragic labyrinth of the general reactions of Algerian society with respect to the problem of the fight against illness, conceived of as an aspect of the French presence. We shall then see in the course of the fight for liberation the crystallization of the new attitude adopted by the Algerian people in respect to medical techniques.

The Visit to the Doctor

The colonized person who goes to see the doctor is always diffident. He answers in monosyllables, gives little in the way of explanation, and soon arouses the doctor's impatience. This attitude is not to be confused with the kind of inhibiting fear that patients usually feel in the doctor's presence. We often hear it said that a certain doctor has a good bedside manner, that he puts his patients at ease. But it so happens that in the colonial situation the personal approach, the ability to be oneself, of establishing and maintaining a "contact," are not observable. The colonial situation standardizes relations, for it dichotomizes the colonial society in a marked way.

The doctor rather quickly gave up the hope of obtaining information from the colonized patient and fell back on the clinical examination, thinking that the body would be more eloquent. But the body proved to be equally rigid. The muscles were contracted. There was no relaxing. Here was the entire man, here was the colonized, facing both a technician and a colonizer.[2] One must, of course, lend an ear to the observations made by the European doctors who examined the patients. But one must also hear those of the patients themselves when they left the hospital. Whereas the *doctors* say: "The pain in their case is protopathic, poorly differentiated, diffuse as in an animal, it is a general malaise rather than a localized pain"; the *patients* say: "They asked me what was wrong with me, as if I were the doctor; they think they're smart and they aren't even able to tell where I feel pain, and the minute you come in they ask you what is wrong with you . . ."

The doctors say: "Those people are rough and unmannerly." The patients say: "I don't trust them." Whereas the doctors claim that the colonized patient doesn't know what he wants, whether to stay sick or be cured, the native keeps saying, "I know how to get into their hospital, but I don't know how I'll get out—*if* I get out." Fairly soon the doctor, and even the nurse, worked out a rule of action: with these people you couldn't practice medicine, you had to be a veterinarian.[3] But finally, by sheer persistence, the doctor would more or less get an idea of what the disease was and prescribe a treatment, which would sometimes not be followed. Sociologists would thereupon venture an explanation and classify all these actions under the heading of fatalism.

The analysis of this pattern of behavior within the colonial framework enables us, on the contrary, to come to other conclusions.

When the colonized escapes the doctor, and the integrity of

[2] This particular observation is related to the overall attitude of the colonized who is hardly ever truthful before the colonizer. The colonized does not let on, does not confess himself, in the presence of the colonizer. The reader is referred to the communication before the 1955 Congress of French-language Psychiatrists and Neurologists on "The Algerian and Avowal in Medico-Legal Practice."

[3] There are obviously a certain number of doctors who act normally, who are human. But of them it will be said: "They are not like the others."

his body is preserved, he considers himself the victor by a handsome margin. For the native the visit is always an ordeal. When the advantage assumed by the colonizer is limited to swallowing pills or potions, the colonized has the impression of having won a victory over the enemy. The end of the visit puts an end to the confrontation. The medicines, the advice, are but the sequels of the ordeal. As for fatalism, a father's apparent refusal, for example, to admit that he owes his son's life to the colonizer's operation, must be studied in two lights. There is, first of all, the fact that the colonized person, who in this respect is like the men in underdeveloped countries or the disinherited in all parts of the world, perceives life not as a flowering or a development of an essential productiveness, but as a permanent struggle against an omnipresent death. This ever-menacing death is experienced as endemic famine, unemployment, a high death rate, an inferiority complex and the absence of any hope for the future.

All this gnawing at the existence of the colonized tends to make of life something resembling an incomplete death. Acts of refusal or rejection of medical treatment are not a refusal of life, but a greater passivity before that close and contagious death. Seen from another angle, this absence of enlightened behavior reveals the colonized native's mistrust of the colonizing technician. The technician's words are always understood in a pejorative way. The truth objectively expressed is constantly vitiated by the lie of the colonial situation.

Medical Supervision, Treatment and the "Double-Power"

A poor subject in the doctor's office, the colonized Algerian proves to be an equally unsatisfactory patient. The colonizing doctor finds that his patient cannot be depended upon to take his medicine regularly, that he takes the wrong doses, fails to appreciate the importance of periodic visits, and takes a paradoxical, frivolous attitude toward the prescribed diet. These are only the most striking and the most common peculiarities that he notes. Hence the general impression that the patient plays hide-and-seek with his doctor. The doctor has no hold on the patient. He finds that in spite of promises and pledges, an attitude of flight, of disengagement persists. All the efforts exerted by the doctor, by his team of nurses, to modify this state of things encounter, not a systematic opposition, but a "vanishing" on the part of the patient.

The first thing that happens is that the patient does not return. This in spite of the fact that it has been clearly explained to him that his ailment, in order to be cured, requires that he be examined several times at given intervals. This is clearly written out in the prescription, it has been explained to him and re-explained, and he has been given a definite appointment with the doctor for a fixed date. But the doctor waits for him in vain. The patient does not arrive. When he does come back, there is the rather shocking discovery that the malady has become very much aggravated. The patient, in fact, comes back five to six months or sometimes a year later. Worse still, he has failed to take the prescribed medicine. An interview with the patient reveals that the medicine was taken only once, or, as often happens, that the amount prescribed for one month was absorbed in a single dose. It may be worth while to dwell on this type of case, for the explanations of it that have been given appear to us quite unsatisfactory.

The sociological theory is that the "native" entertains the firm hope of being cured once and for all. The native, in fact, sees the ailment, not as progressing little by little but as assaulting the individual in a single swoop, so that the effectiveness of a remedy would not depend so much on its consistent, periodic, and progressive repetition but on its total impact, its immediate effect; this accounts for the natives' preference for injections. According to this theory, the doctor would always have to heal at a single sitting. Pilgrimages to a sanctuary, the making of amulets or marks written on a piece of paper—these are therapies that are applied immediately with the maximum effectiveness. Just as neglecting a ritual duty or transgressing a given taboo causes the disease to break out, so performing certain actions or following the medicine man's or the sorcerer's prescriptions are capable of expelling the disease and restoring the equilibrium between the different forces that govern the life of the group.

This explanation surely contains an element of truth. But it seems to us, to interpret a phenomenon arising out of the colonial situation in terms of patterns of conduct existing before the foreign conquest, even if this phenomenon is analagous to certain traditional patterns, is nevertheless in certain respects false. Colonial domination, as we have seen, gives rise to and continues to dictate a whole complex of resentful behavior and of refusal on the part of the colonized. The colonized exerts a considerable effort to keep away from the colonial world, not to expose himself to any action of the conqueror. In everyday life, however, the colonized and the colonizers are constantly establishing bonds of economic, technical, and administrative dependence. Colonialism obviously throws all the elements of native society into confusion. The dominant group arrives with its values and imposes them with such violence that the very life of the colonized can manifest itself only defensively, in a more or less clandestine way. Under these conditions, colonial domination distorts the very relations that the colonized maintains with his own culture. In a great number of cases, the practice of tradition is a disturbed practice, the colonized being unable to reject completely modern discoveries and the arsenal of weapons against diseases possessed by the hospitals, the ambulances, the nurses. But the colonized who accepts the intervention of medical technique, if he does not go to the hospital, will be subjected to considerable pressure on the part of his group. The traditional methods of treatment are applied in addition to the modern medical technique. "Two remedies are better than one." It must be remembered that the colonized who accepts penicillin or digitalin at the same time insists on following the treatment prescribed by the healer of his village or his district.

The colonized obscurely realizes that penicillin is more effective, but for political, psychological, social reasons, he must at the same time give traditional medicine its due. (The healer fulfills a function and therefore needs to earn a living.) Psychologically, the colonized has difficulty, even here in the presence of illness, in rejecting the habits of his group and the reactions of his culture. Accepting the medicine, even once, is admitting, to a limited extent perhaps but nonetheless ambiguously, the validity of the Western technique. It is demonstrating one's confidence in the foreigner's medical science. Swallowing the whole dose in one gulp is literally getting even with it.

To gradually adopt an almost obsessional respect for the colonizer's prescription often proves difficult. The other power, in fact, intervenes and breaks the unifying circle of the Western therapy. Every pill absorbed or every injection taken invites the application of a preparation or the visit to a saint. Sometimes the patient gives evidence of the fear of being the battleground for different and opposed forces. This fear gives rise to important stresses and the whole picture of the illness is thereby modified. Once again, the colonial world reveals itself to be complex and extremely diverse in structure. There is always an opposition of exclusive worlds, a contradictory interaction of different techniques, a vehement confrontation of values.

The Colonized and the Native Doctor

The colonial situation does not only vitiate the relations between doctor and patient. We have shown that the doctor always appears as a link in the colonialist network, as a spokesman for the occupying power. We shall see that this ambivalence of the patient before medical technique is to be found even when the doctor belongs to the dominated people. There is a manifest ambivalence of the colonized group with respect to any member who acquires a technique or the manners of the conqueror. For the group, in fact, the native technician is living proof that any one of its members is capable of being an engineer, a lawyer or a doctor. But there is at the same time, in the background, the awareness of a sudden divergence between the homogeneous group, enclosed within itself, and this native technician who has escaped beyond the specific psychological or emotional categories of the people. The native doctor is a Europeanized, Westernized doctor, and in certain circumstances he is considered as no longer being a part of the dominated society. He is tacitly rejected into the camp of the oppressors, into the opposing camp. It is not by accident that in certain colonies the educated native is referred to as "having acquired the habits of a master."

For many of the colonized, the native doctor is compared to the native police, to the *caïd,* to the notable. The colonized is both proud of the success of his *race* and at the same time looks upon this technician with disapproval. The native doctor's behavior with respect to the traditional medicine of his country is for a long time characterized by a considerable aggressiveness.

The native doctor feels himself psychologically compelled to demonstrate firmly his new admission to a rational universe. This accounts for the abrupt way in which he rejects the magic practices of his people. Given the ambivalence of the colonized with respect to the native doctor and the ambivalence of the native doctor before certain features of his culture, the encounter of doctor and patient inevitably proves difficult. The colonized patient is the first to set the tone. Once the superiority of Western technique over traditional methods of treatment is recognized, it is thought preferable to turn to the colonizers who are, after all, "the true possessors of the technique." As far as practice goes, it is common to see European doctors receiving both Algerian and European patients, whereas Algerian doctors generally receive only Algerians. Some exceptions could of course be mentioned; but on the whole, this description is valid for Algeria. The native doctor, because of the operation of the complex psychological laws that govern colonial society, frequently finds himself in a difficult position.

We are dealing here with the drama of the colonized intellectuals *before* the fight for liberation. We shall soon see what important modifications have been introduced into Algeria by the national war of liberation.

The European Doctor During the Struggle for Liberation

Generally speaking, the colonizing doctor adopts the attitude of his group toward the struggle of the Algerian people. Behind "the doctor who heals the wounds of humanity" appears the man, a member of a dominant society and enjoying in Algeria the benefit of an incomparably higher standard of living than that of his metropolitan colleague.[4]

Moreover, in centers of colonization the doctor is nearly always a landowner as well. It is exceptional to see in Algeria, a colony which attracts settlers, a doctor who does not take up farming, who does not become attached to the soil. Whether the land has come to him from his family, or he has bought it himself, the doctor is a settler. The European population in Algeria has not yet clearly marked out for itself the different sectors of economic life. Colonial society is a mobile society, poorly structured, and the European, even when he is a technician, always assumes a certain degree of polyvalence. In the heart of every European in the colonies there slumbers a man of energy, a pioneer, an adventurer. Not even the civil servant transferred for two years to a colonial territory fails to feel himself psychologically changed in certain respects.

The European individual in Algeria does not take his place

[4] Medical practice in the colonies very often assumes an aspect of systematized piracy. Injections of twice-distilled water, billed as penicillin or vitamin B-12, chest X-rays, radiotherapy sessions "to stabilize a cancer," given by a doctor who has no radiological equipment, are examples. In the latter case, the doctor need only place the patient behind a sheet and after 15 or 20 minutes announce that the session is over. It even happens that doctors in rural centers (several examples of this in Algeria are known) boast of taking X-rays with the aid of a vacuum cleaner. We may mention the case of a European doctor practicing in Rabelais (in the region of Orléansville) who explains how he manages, on market days, to earn more than 30,000 francs in the course of a morning. "I fill three syringes of unequal size with salt serum and I say to the patient, 'Which injection do you want, the 500, the 1000 or the 1500 franc one?' The patient," so the doctor explains, "almost always chooses the most expensive injection."

in a structured and relatively stable society. The colonial society is in perpetual movement. Every settler invents a new society, sets up or sketches new structures. The differences between craftsmen, civil servants, workers, and professionals are poorly defined. Every doctor has his vineyards and the lawyer busies himself with his rice fields as passionately as any settler. The doctor is not socially defined by the exercise of his profession alone. He is likewise the owner of mills, wine cellars, or orange groves, and he coyly speaks of his medicine as simply a supplementary source of income. Not exclusively dependent on his practice, deriving a sometimes enormous income from his properties, the doctor has a certain conception of professional morality and of medical practice. The colonialist arrogance, the contempt for the client, the hateful brutality toward the indigent are more or less contained in the formula, "I don't have to sit around waiting for clients to make a living." The doctor in Besançon, in Liège, or in Basel has left the land and has taken his place in the economic sector defined by his profession. Perpetually in contact with suffering humanity, the world of the sick and the disabled, the doctor has a set of values. Thus he will usually be found to belong to one of the democratic parties, and his ideas are likely to be anticolonialist. In the colonies, the doctor is an integral part of colonization, of domination, of exploitation. In Algeria we must not be surprised to find that doctors and professors of medicine are leaders of colonialist movements.

The Algerian doctor is economically interested in the maintenance of colonial oppression. This is not a question of values or of principles, but of the incomparably high standard of living that the colonial situation provides him. This explains the fact that very often he assumes the role of militia chief or organizer of "counter-terrorist" raids. In the colonies, in normal times—that is, in the absence of the war of liberation—there is something of the cowboy and the pioneer even in the intellectual. In a period of crisis the cowboy pulls out his revolver and his instruments of torture.

In this frightful war that is bathing Algeria in blood, an effort is required to understand certain facts, objectively distressing in a normal situation. The murder of certain doctors in Algeria has never been clearly understood by world opinion. In the cruelest wars, it is traditional for the medical corps to be left unscathed. For example in 1944, while freeing a village in the region of Belfort, we left a guard at the entrance to a school where German surgeons were operating on the wounded. The Algerian political men are quite aware of the existence of laws of war. They know the complexity of the problem and the dramatic situation of the European population. How is one to explain those cases, the decisions made to take the life of a doctor?

It is almost always because the doctor himself, by his behavior, has decided to exclude himself from the protective circle that the principles and the values of the medical profession have woven around him. The doctor who is killed in Algeria, in isolated cases, is always a war criminal. In a colonial situation there are special realities. In a given region, the doctor sometimes reveals himself as the most sanguinary of colonizers. His identity as a doctor no longer matters. Just as he was a doctor in addition to being a property owner, so he becomes the torturer who happens to be a doctor. The dominant authority, for that matter, has organized the over-all behavior of the doctor as it relates to the struggle for liberation. Thus, any doctor treating an Algerian whose wound appears suspicious must, on penalty of legal action, take down the name of the patient, his address, the names of those accompanying him, their address, and communicate the information to the authorities.[5]

[5] With respect to these measures the Council of the Order of Doctors in France adopted a very firm position consistent with the great French tradition.

Thus, its President, Professor Piedelièvre, in an official letter addressed to the Councils of the Order of Doctors of Algiers, of Constantine, and of Oran wrote: "May I remind you that in no case and under no pretext can professional secrecy be violated! I likewise point out to you that doctors are duty bound to treat all persons with the same conscientiousness, whatever be their religion or their race, whether they are friends or enemies. I wish to draw your attention, finally, to the fact that the Code

As for the pharmacists, they were to be given orders not to deliver without a medical prescription such drugs as penicillin, streptomycin, antibiotics in general, alcohol, absorbent cotton, anti-tetanus serum. Moreover, they were strongly urged to note down the identity and the address of the patient.

As soon as they were known to the people, these measures confirmed their certainty that the colonizers were in complete agreement to fight against them. Convinced that the European doctors and pharmacists would comply with this decision, the French authorities posted police officers in civilian clothes or informers in the vicinity of the pharmacies run by Algerians. The supplying of medicines in certain areas became a difficult and painful problem. Alcohol, sulpha drugs, syringes were refused. In 1955, the French military command in its estimates of Algerian losses nearly always included a certain number of hypothetically wounded who, "for lack of treatment are assumed dead."

The colonizing doctor, meanwhile, emphasized his membership in the dominating society by certain attitudes. When judicial inquiries into the cases of Algerians who had not died in the course of police questioning began, it would happen that the defense would ask for a medico-legal examination. This demand would sometimes be met. The European doctor assigned to examine the patient always concluded that there was no evidence to suggest that the accused had been tortured. A few times, early in 1955, Algerians were appointed as experts. But precise instructions prohibiting this were soon issued. Likewise, if it happened that a European doctor noted "the existence of elements that might suggest the hypothesis that acts described by the accused produced his wounds," another expert opinion was immediately found to contradict him. Obviously, such a

---

of Deontology, in its Article Three, has clearly stated: '*The doctor must treat all his patients with the same conscientiousness, whatever be their condition, their nationality, their religion, their reputation and his feeling toward them.*'" We may add further that many European doctors refused to apply the decisions adopted by the French authorities in Algeria.

doctor was never called in again. Not infrequently the European doctor in Algeria would deliver to the legal authority a certificate of natural death for an Algerian who had succumbed to torture or who, more simply, had been coldly executed. Similarly, it invariably happened that when the demand of the defense for an autopsy was granted, the results would be negative.

On the strictly technical level, the European doctor actively collaborates with the colonial forces in their most frightful and most degrading practices. We should like to mention here some of the practices engaged in by the European medical corps in Algeria, which shed light on certain "murders" of doctors.

First of all, the "truth serum." The principle of this drug is well known: a chemical substance having hypnotic properties is injected into a vein, which, when the operation is carried out slowly, produces a certain loss of control, a blunting of consciousness. As a therapeutic measure used in medicine it is obviously a very dangerous technique, which may cause a serious impairment of the personality. Many psychiatrists, considering the dangers greater than the possible improvements, have long ago abandoned this technique for examining spheres of the unconscious.

All the Academies of Medicine of all the countries in the world have formally condemned the use of this practice for legal ends and the doctor who violates these solemn proscriptions is obviously contemptuous of the fundamental principles of medicine. The doctor who fights side by side with his people, as a doctor, must respect the international charter of his profession. A criminal doctor, in all countries in the world, is sentenced to death. The example of the doctors in the human experimentation camps of the Nazis is particularly edifying.

The European doctors in Algeria use the "truth serum" with staggering frequency. We may recall here the experience of Henri Alleg, as related in *The Question*.[6]

We have had occasion to treat men and women who had been

[6] H. Alleg, *La Question*, Editions de Minuit, 1958.

subjected to this torture for days. We shall study elsewhere the grave consequences of these practices, but we can point out here that the most important consequence has appeared to us to be a certain inability to distinguish the true from the false, and an almost obsessive fear of saying what should remain hidden. We must always remember that there is hardly an Algerian who is not a party to at least one secret of the Revolution. Months after this torture, the former prisoner hesitates to say his name, the town where he was born. Every question is first experienced as a repetition of the torturer-tortured relationship.

Other doctors, attached to the various torture centers, intervene after every session in order to put the tortured back into condition for new sessions. Under the circumstances, the important thing is for the prisoner not to give the slip to the team in charge of the questioning: in other words, to remain alive. Everything—heart stimulants, massive doses of vitamins—is used before, during, and after the sessions to keep the Algerian hovering between life and death. Ten times the doctor intervenes, ten times he gives the prisoner back to the pack of torturers.

In the European medical corps in Algeria, and especially in the military health corps, such things are common. Professional morality, medical ethics, self-respect and respect for others, have given way to the most uncivilized, the most degrading, the most perverse kinds of behavior. Finally, attention must be called to the habit formed by certain psychiatrists of flying to the aid of the police. There are, for instance, psychiatrists in Algiers, known to numerous prisoners, who have given electric shock treatments to the accused and have questioned them during the waking phase, which is characterized by a certain confusion, a relaxation of resistance, a disappearance of the person's defenses. When by chance these men are liberated because the doctor, despite this barbarous treatment, was able to obtain no information, what is brought to us is a personality in shreds. The work of rehabilitating the man is then extremely difficult.

This is only one of the numerous crimes of which French colonialism in Algeria has made itself guilty.[7]

The Algerian People, Medical Technique and the War of Liberation

We have had occasion many times to point out the appearance of radically new types of behavior in various aspects of the private and public life of the Algerian. The shock that broke the chains of colonialism has moderated exclusive attitudes, reduced extreme positions, made certain arbitrary views obsolete. Medical science and concern for one's health have always been proposed or imposed by the occupying power. In the colonial situation, however, it is impossible to create the physical and psychological conditions for the learning of hygiene or for the assimilation of concepts concerning epidemic diseases. In the colonial situation, going to see the doctor, the administrator, the constable or the mayor are identical moves. The sense of alienation from colonial society and the mistrust of the representatives of its authority, are always accompanied by an almost mechanical sense of detachment and mistrust of even the things that are most positive and most profitable to the population.

We have noted that in the very first months of the struggle, the French authorities decided to put an embargo on antibiotics, ether, alcohol, anti-tetanus vaccine. The Algerian who wished to obtain any of these medications was required to give the pharmacist detailed information as to his identity and that of the patient. Just when the Algerian people decided no longer to wait for others to treat them, colonialism prohibited the sale of medications and surgical instruments. Just when the Algerian was set to live and take care of himself, the occupying power

[7] We have seen military doctors, called to the bedside of an Algerian soldier wounded in combat, refuse to treat him. The official pretext was that there was no longer a chance to save the wounded man. After the soldier had died, the doctor would admit that this solution had appeared to him preferable to a stay in prison where it would have been necessary to feed him while awaiting execution. The Algerians of the region of Blida know a certain hospital director who would kick the bleeding chests of the war wounded lying in the corridor of his establishment.

doomed him to a horrible agony. Numerous families had to stand by powerless, their hearts full of rancor, and watch the atrocious death by tetanus of wounded *moudjahidines* who had taken refuge in their houses. From the earliest months of the Revolution, the directives of the National Front were clearly given: any wound, no matter how benign, automatically required an anti-tetanus vaccine injection. This the people knew. And when the wound, ugly to look at, had been cleaned of the dirt and grit picked up in the course of the retreat, the comrades of the wounded man would suddenly be seized with the fear of a tetanus infection. But the pharmacists were adamant: the sale of anti-tetanus vaccine was prohibited. Dozens and dozens of Algerians today can describe the slow, frightful death of a wounded man, progressively paralyzed, then twisted, and again paralyzed by the tetanus toxin. No one remains in the room to the end, they say in conclusion.

Yet the Algerian, when he sometimes would get a European to make his purchases, would see him return with the medicine which he had obtained without difficulty. The same Algerian had previously begged all the pharmacists of the vicinity, and had finally given up, having felt the last pharmacist's hard and inquisitorial eye on him. The European would return, loaded down with medicines, relaxed, innocent. Such experiences have not made it easy for the Algerian to keep a balanced judgment toward members of the European minority. Science depoliticized, science in the service of man, is often non-existent in the colonies. For this Algerian who for hours has begged unsuccessfully for a hundred grams of sterile cotton, the colonialist world constitutes a monolithic block. Alcohol being similarly prohibited, the wounds would be dressed with lukewarm water and, for lack of ether, amputations would be carried out without anaesthetics.

Now all these things that could not be found, that were held by the adversary, withdrawn from circulation, were to take on a new value. These medications which were taken for granted before the struggle for liberation, were transformed into weapons. And the urban revolutionary cells having the responsibility for supplying medications were as important as those assigned to obtain information as to the plans and movements of the adversary. Even as the Algerian tradesman discovered ways of supplying the people with radios, so the Algerian pharmacist, the Algerian nurse, the Algerian doctor multiplied their efforts to make antibiotics and dressings available to the wounded at all times. From Tunisia and Morocco, finally, during the crucial months of 1956 and 1957, was to come a steady flow of medical supplies that saved an incalculable number of human lives.

The development of the war in Algeria, the setting up of units of the National Army of Liberation throughout the territory, brought about a dramatic public health problem. The increase in the number of areas constituting a threat to the adversary led him to interrupt regular activities, such as the visit of the doctor to the *douars*. From one day to the next, the population was left to shift for itself, and the National Liberaion Front had to take drastic measures. It found itself faced with the necessity of setting up a system of public health capable of replacing the periodic visit of the colonial doctor. This is how the local cell member responsible for health became an important member of the revolutionary apparatus. The problem, moreover, became more and more complex. Bombardments and raids on civilians were now added to natural diseases. It is a known fact that for one Algerian soldier hit, there are ten civilians killed or wounded. There is no lack of testimony from French soldiers to this effect. Under such circumstances, medical supplies and technicians became indispensable. It was during this period that orders were given to medical students, nurses, and doctors to join the combatants. Meetings were organized among political leaders and health technicians. After a short time, people's delegates assigned to handle public health problems came and joined each cell. All questions were dealt with in a remarkable spirit of revolutionary solidarity.

There was no paternalism; there was no timidity. On the contrary, a concerted effort was made to achieve the health plan that had been worked out. The health technician did not launch a "psychological approach program for the purpose of winning over the underdeveloped population." The problem was, under the direction of the national authority, to supervise the people's health, to protect the lives of our women, of our children, of our combatants.

We must dwell on the new reality that the rise of a national power has constituted in Algeria since 1954. This national authority has taken upon itself the responsibility for the health of the people, and the people have abandoned their old passivity. The people involved in this fight against death have shown exceptional conscientiousness and enthusiasm in their observance of the directives.

The Algerian doctor, the native doctor who, as we have seen, was looked upon before the national combat as an ambassador of the occupier, was reintegrated into the group. Sleeping on the ground with the men and women of the *mechtas,* living the drama of the people, the Algerian doctor became a part of the Algerian body. There was no longer that reticence, so constant during the period of unchallenged oppression. He was no longer "the" doctor, but "our" doctor, "our" technician.

The people henceforth demanded and practiced a technique stripped of its foreign characteristics. The war of liberation introduced medical technique and the native technician into the life of innumerable regions of Algeria. Populations accustomed to the monthly or biennial visits of European doctors saw Algerian doctors settling permanently in their villages. The Revolution and medicine manifested their presence simultaneously.

It is understandable that such facts should provide the basis for an incomparable dynamism and the point of departure for new attitudes. The problems of hygiene and of prevention of disease were approached in a remarkably creative atmosphere. The latrines recommended by the colonial administration had not been accepted in the *mechtas* but they were now installed in great numbers. Ideas on the transmission of intestinal parasites were immediately assimilated by the people. The elimination of stagnant pools was undertaken and the fight against post-natal ophthalmia achieved spectacular results. The problem was no longer that mothers neglected their children, but that aureomycin was at times unavailable. The people wanted to get well, wanted to care for themselves and were anxious to understand the explanations proffered by fellow doctors or nurses.[8] Schools for nurses were opened and the illiterate, in a few days, proved capable of making intravenous injections.

Similarly, old superstitions began to crumble. Witchcraft, *maraboutism* (already considerably discredited as a result of the propaganda carried on by the intellectuals), belief in the *djinn,* all these things that seemed to be part of the very being of the Algerian, were swept away by the action and practice initiated by the Revolution.[9] Even instructions difficult for highly technological societies to accept were assimilated by the Algerian. We shall give two significant examples of this.

First of all, a rule was made against giving a drink of water to a man wounded in the abdomen. Instructions were categorical. Lectures were given to the people. Not a boy, not a girl must be

[8] A change in attitude on the part of the Algerian toward the occupier's hospital centers was likewise to be noted. It would in fact happen that the need of a particular medication or of a surgical operation impossible to carry out in the maquis would cause the doctor to advise the civilian to let himself be transferred to a hospital directed by the French. The hesitations and refusals that had been met with before the Revolution vanished and the population would follow the orders given by the Algerian doctor in the maquis. This new attitude was very marked in 1956-57. I had occasion during this period to visit a great number of hospitals. The European doctors expressed their surprise to me at the time. Since the war, they said, "the Moslems let themselves be treated in the hospitals in the proportion of five to one as compared to the preceding years. One wonders why this is so." It should also be added that the hospital administrations in the maquis had a strategic interest in having civilians cared for by the French and keeping medical supplies for the soldiers, who could not be evacuated.

[9] *maraboutism*—the practice of medicine by the *marabout,* the Moslem priest. (Translator's note)

The *djinn* (plural *djnoun*) is a spirit. He haunts the houses and the fields. Popular belief attributed to him an important role in all the phenomena of life: birth, circumcision, marriage, sickness, death. In the case of disease, any impairment of health was interpreted as the work of a bad *djinn.*

allowed to remain uninformed as to this rule: never a drop of water to a soldier wounded in the belly. After a battle, while awaiting the arrival of a doctor, the people gathered round the wounded would listen without weakening to the entreaties of the combatant. For hours, the women would obstinately refuse the wounded the requested swallow of water. And even the *moudjahid's* own son did not hesitate to say to his father, "Here is your gun, kill me if you want, but I will not give you the water you ask for." When the doctor arrived, the necessary operation would be performed, and the *moudjahid* would have the maximum chance of recovering.

The second example relates to the strict diet to be followed in the course of a typhus infection. In the hospital the observance of the rules is obtained by the prohibition of family visits. For experience has shown that whenever a member of the family is allowed to visit the patient he lets himself be moved by the typhus patient's "hunger" and manages to leave him some cakes or some chicken. The result is that often an intestinal perforation results.

In the colonial situation, these things assume a special significance, for the colonized interprets this medical injunction as a new form of torture, of famine, a new manifestation of the occupant's inhuman methods. If the typhus patient is a child, one can understand the feelings that can overcome the mother. Out in the *djebel,* on the other hand, the Algerian nurse or doctor is able to win the patient's family over to a complete cooperation: hygienic precautions, regular administration of medications, prohibition of visits, isolation, and strict observance of diet for several days. The Algerian mother, who had never in her life seen a doctor, would follow the technician's instructions to the letter.

Specialists in basic health education should give careful thought to the new situations that develop in the course of a struggle for national liberation on the part of an underdeveloped people. Once the body of the nation begins to live again in a coherent and dynamic way, everything becomes possible. The notions about "native psychology" or of the "basic personality" are shown to be vain. The people who take their destiny into their own hands assimilate the most modern forms of technology at an extraordinary rate.

5

Algeria's European Minority[1]

In the preceding pages we have on several occasions tried to shed light on certain aspects of Algeria's European society. We have drawn attention to the often odious behavior of certain Europeans. One would of course have liked to find among Algeria's European doctors and intellectuals a desire to lessen the tension, to facilitate contacts, to play down the conflict. We know that, instead, European intellectuals have taken over the colonists' cause. The Sérignys, the Borgeauds, the Laquières[2] have disappeared or operate in the background. Nor must it be imagined that they act through intermediaries. That period is now closed. The Lagaillardes and the Regards[3] are not straw men. They have assumed the leadership of the colonialist forces, made direct contacts with the army and the French parties of the right, and do not rule out the possibility of a sudden break from France. The traditionalists of colonization have long ago been outdistanced. Accustomed to parliamentary action, to political pressures, and to backstage maneuvering, these men in the past three months have shown a marked hesitation. This is because the new kingpins of the colonization see the future in apocalyptic terms. Some of Algeria's European intellectuals, because they have links with the colonial power, have often contributed to giving the Algerian war its hallucinatory character.

[1] First published in *Les Temps Modernes,* June, 1959.

[2] Sérigny, Borgeaud, Laquière—leading figures among the French colonists.

[3] Lagaillarde, Regard—young activist leaders.

We have seen doctors assigned full time to the dispensaries of the judicial police, and we know that philosophers and priests, in the relocation or internment centers, assume the mission of brain-washing, of probing souls, of making the Algerian man unrecognizable.

But we shall see that Algeria's European minority is far from being the monolithic block that one imagines. Mr. Laffont, the director of the newspaper *L'Echo d'Oran,* in declaring recently that Algiers does not represent Algeria, in fact manifests the desire that certain Europeans feel to keep their distance from the colonialist General Staff of Algiers. One could go further and say that the rue Michelet, the rue d'Isly, and a few cafés of Bab-el-Oued do not represent Algeria.[4]

In April 1953, at a meeting of the Board of Directors of the M.T.L.D.,[5] the decision was reached to establish contact with the European population and to initiate exchanges of views with the main groups representing the interests of the European minority. The U.D.M.A. likewise, in its doctrinal publications, constantly reminded its militants of the strategic and political necessity of not consigning all the Europeans to the colonialist side.[6] We may mention, incidently, that several Europeans were at that time members of the U.D.M.A.

Such positions were rapidly to bring rewards. In the cities, more and more meetings were held between Moslem Algerians and European Algerians. These meetings had nothing in common with the Franco-Moslem forces of the colonialist authorities. There was no *méchoui,* no exoticism, no paternalism or humility.[7] Men and women discussed their future, called attention to the dangers that beset their country.

Groups of young people would meet during this period, and

[4] The rue Michelet, the rue d'Isly—in the heart of the business center of Algiers; Bab-el-Oued—popular district frequented by Europeans.

[5] M.T.L.D.—Movement for the Triumph of Democratic Liberties. An Algerian nationalist party formed before the Revolution. (Translator's note)

[6] U.D.M.A.—Democratic Union of the Algerian Manifesto. Another Algerian nationalist party. (Translator's note)

[7] *Méchoui*—traditional Arab mutton dish. (Translator's note)

outings were organized. Associations of girls joined hands and began to work together; the psychological bases for human and really democratic encounters were definitely laid.

Europeans who were known or supposed to be democrats and anti-colonialists were approached by the leaders. The Algerian question was studied from all angles, and very often, after a complete survey of the colonial situation, the Europeans would be the ones to express surprise that Algeria had not yet drawn the conclusions to which the political failures pointed. Very often these Europeans would themselves reach the realization of the necessity for armed action as the only means of rescuing Algeria from its desperate situation.

It has often been claimed that the F.L.N. made no distinction among the different members of Algeria's European society. Those who make such accusations fail to take into account both the policy long defined by the Front with respect to Algeria's Europeans, and the constant support that hundreds and hundreds of European men and women have brought to our units and to our political cells. What we have said is that the Algerian people are spontaneously aware of the importance of the European population which expresses itself through its oppressive system and especially through the silence and inactivity of the French democrats in Algeria in the face of the affirmed and total violence of the colonialists.

Other things being equal, it can be said of Algeria's European democrats what has been endlessly repeated of the French parties of the Left: for a long time history is made without them. They were unable to prevent the sending of contingents to Algeria, unable to prevent Guy Mollet's capitulation. They were passive under Lacoste, powerless before the military coup of the 13th of May. Nevertheless, their existence has forced the neo-fascists of Algeria and France to be on the defensive. *The Left has done nothing for a long time in France.* Yet by its action, its denunciations, and its analyses, it has prevented a certain number of things.

Algeria's European democrats, in the framework of the Algerian war, could not as a whole act like their homologues living in France. Democracy in France traditionally lives in broad daylight. In Algeria, democracy is tantamount to treason. A Claude Bourdet, a Domenach, a Pierre Cot can publicly take a position different from that of the government of their country. Being former members of the resistance, having from the beginning devoted their lives to the defense and to the triumph of certain principles, they experience no hesitation. And the threats, when they come, do not budge them. But we must emphasize the fact that within the framework of the French hexagon, democratic traditions have by and large been maintained. France, as an imperialist country, has great racist potentialities, as we have seen more clearly in the past two years, but among Frenchmen there are reflexes that operate spontaneously. This accounts for the relative freedom left to opponents—less and less, however, because France is beginning to be colonized by the Algerian activists—and this also accounts for the outburst of public indignation that greets every revelation that reaches France regarding the tortures practiced in Algeria.

Because of their own contradictions and because of the power and the radicalism of the reactionary parties, the forces of the Left in France have up to the present time been unable to impose negotiation. But undeniably they are constantly forcing the extremists to unmask themselves, and hence progressively to adopt the positions that will precipitate their defeat.

In Algeria the forces of the Left do not exist. It is unthinkable for European democrats really to militate in Algeria outside the Algerian Communist Party. We know that even the Algerian Communist Party was for a long time confined within a reformist position of the French Union type, and that for long months after November 1, 1954, the Algerian Communists denounced the *terroristes provocateurs*—in other words, the F.L.N.

Algeria's European democrats have from the beginning lived in a more or less clandestine state. Drowned in the European mass, they live in a world of values that their principles reject and condemn. The European democrat is on the defensive. He has contacts with Algerians but in secrecy. In the European colony he is referred to as "the Arab." All these phenomena are well known, and they have appeared in Indochina, in Africa south of the Sahara, in Tunisia, and in Morocco.

This democratic European, accustomed to semi-clandestine contacts with Algerians, unwittingly learns the laws of revolutionary action. And when those whom he used to receive in his home tell him to give shelter to a friend, to find medications, or to transport a parcel, there is as a rule no difficulty. We must emphasize the point that never has a member of the Front deceived a French democrat. It would be out of the question to expose a man or a woman who had always commanded our esteem to the slightest risk, without warning them. The decision to help the F.L.N. was taken quite knowingly, in a wholly responsible way. Never has a French democrat been deceived. Sometimes, especially in the extremely crucial periods of 1957, it would happen that a democrat would hold back and refuse, in despair, the service requested; but never was there an attempt to deceive or to exploit the sincerity and the good will of the Europeans.

It should perhaps be added that often the European would ask not to be told the details of the matter in connection with which his collaboration was being sought. But the leadership was uncompromising as to this. The F.L.N. wanted responsible people, not people who at the slightest hitch would break down and claim that they had been deceived.

The European men and women who have been arrested and tortured by the police services and the French parachutists, by their attitude under torture, have shown the rightness of this position taken by the F.L.N. Not a single Frenchman has revealed to the colonialist police information vital to the Revolution. On the contrary, the arrested Europeans have resisted long enough to enable the other members of the network to disappear. The tortured European has behaved like an authentic militant in the national fight for independence.

For five years the F.L.N. has not considered it necessary to insist on the participation of Europeans in the fight for liberation. This policy is dictated by the consideration that these Europeans should not be made conspicuous, that their action should not be differentiated from that of any other Algerian. The F.L.N. did not want to make of them "show Europeans" in the ranks of the Revolution, on the model of colonial Algeria where the "show" Moslem and Jew were ritually to be found in every committee.

For the F.L.N., in the new society that is being built, there are only Algerians. From the outset, therefore, every individual living in Algeria is an Algerian. In tomorrow's independent Algeria it will be up to every Algerian to assume Algerian citizenship or to reject it in favor of another.

There are, to be sure, the war criminals, all those torturers spawned by the civil strifes of Saigon, Tunis, or Meknès, and who today in Algiers or in Mascara, before the end of the colonial reign whose approach they sense, are bent on shedding the greatest possible amount of blood. Those men belong nowhere. Now that the French colonial empire is being shaken by its last spasms, the French would do well to identify them. If they return to France, these men should be kept under surveillance. Jackals do not take to feeding on milk overnight. The taste of blood and of crime is deeply embedded in the very being of these creatures who, it should be said, must be retrieved by psychiatry.

There are also the few hundred European colonialists, powerful, intractable, those who have at all times instigated repressions, broken the French democrats, blocked every endeavor within the colonial framework to introduce a modicum of democracy into Algeria.

The Algerian people need not restate their position with respect to these men who have considered Algeria and the Algerians as a private reserve. The people have excluded them from the Algerian nation and they must not hope to be "taken back."

We shall now show in detail that the European minority has

in the past few years become diversified and that considerable numbers of non-Arab Algerians have identified themselves with the Algerian cause and collaborate actively in the struggle, while others officially fight in the ranks of the Algerian Revolution.

Algeria's Jews

The Algerian Jews represent one-fifth of the non-Moslem population of Algeria. Their attitude toward the struggle of the Algerian people is obviously not a homogeneous one. A socio-economic analysis affords a complete explanation of the different attitudes adopted by the members of the Jewish community.

A first group of Jews has bound its fate very closely with that of the colonial domination. Jewish tradesmen, for example, protected against competition from the Algerians by their status as Frenchmen, would not look too favorably upon the setting up of an Algerian national authority and the disappearance of preferential systems. It is a fact that the banks make it enormously difficult for Algerian tradesmen to borrow money and very often block their transactions and thus actively collaborate in their bankruptcy, or in any case limit the expansion of their business and consequently prevent it from becoming a danger to other tradesmen.

In every large city in Algeria, however, one or two Algerians can be found who, by dint of tenacity and business acumen, have managed to circumvent the maneuvers and to constitute a threat to the pre-eminence of the Jewish tradesmen.

"If ever they get their independence," the tradesmen admit, "they will take our place." On the level of economic competition, therefore, there is the fear on the part of the Jewish tradesman that equality in the competition that would be set up by an Algerian power would be prejudicial to him. This fear is far from being the exclusive characteristic of Jewish tradesmen. It is to be found in European tradesmen of all origins, in every business, large and small. The end of the colonial regime is looked upon as the end of prosperity.

It must be pointed out, however, that such a state of mind is not to be found at all levels and in all regions. In the centers where the Jewish tradesman maintains close contacts with the Algerian population and where economic independence is pretty clear, there is a confusion of interests. In these centers, Jewish tradesmen furnish the A.L.N. its supplies of military clothes, blankets. . . .[8] It is no secret that since 1954 several Jewish tradesmen have been arrested for aiding and abetting the Algerian Revolution.

Jewish civil servants, practically the only administrative personnel recruited locally—Algeria's Europeans are settlers or else exercise liberal professions—also look upon the prospect of the birth of an Algerian state with fear and trembling. It is easy for them to guess that the freedom of every Algerian to receive schooling and possibly a scholarship, the disappearance of ostracism and of the *numerus clausus,* would introduce radical modifications in their privileges. One remembers the discontent expressed by European civil servants in Algeria when, in a show of "conscience," the French authorities waved the spectre of "the accession of Moslems to public service."

This state of mind, although frequent in Algeria, does not exclude absolutely opposite positions. We know Jewish police officers who, especially in 1955-56, retarded the arrest of patriots even though it had been ordered on a high level, thus often enabling them to "disappear."

Finally, colonial Algeria being an eminently racist country, the different mechanisms of racist psychology are to be found there. Thus the Jew, despised and excluded by the European, is quite happy on certain occasions to identify himself with those who humiliate him to humiliate the Algerian in turn. But it is very rare, except in the region of Constantine where many poor Jews find shelter in the shadow of the colonial reign, to see Jews, in broad daylight, affirm their membership in Algeria's extremist groups.

Alongside the two large categories of Jewish tradespeople and

[8] A.L.N.—Army of National Liberation. (Translator's note)

civil servants, there is the great majority, a floating, highly Arabized mass having only a poor knowledge of French, considering itself by tradition and sometimes by dress as authentic "natives." This mass represents three-fourths of the Algerian Jewish population. They are in the Algerian territory the homologues of the Tunisian Jews of the Moroccan *Djerba* or the *mellah*.[9] For these Jews, there is no problem: they are Algerians.

We see therefore that the fraction of the Jewish minority actively engaged in the ranks of colonialism is relatively unimportant. Let us now look at the case of Algerian Jews participating in the fight for national liberation.

At the time when the French authorities decided to create urban and rural militias, the Jewish citizens wished to know what attitude to adopt in the face of this mobilization. A few of them did not hesitate to propose to the F.L.N. that, instead of responding to the requisition order, they join the nearest maquis. The Front as a whole advised caution, merely asking these Jews, within the framework of their professions, to become "the eyes and ears of the Revolution" inside the enemy apparatus.

Their presence in the militias, moveover, has rendered service to the struggle. Thus the members of a patrol advise the chiefs of the size of the units, the nature of their arms, the route to be followed, the times when the rounds are made. Likewise the chiefs are often kept informed of reprisal operations organized against this or that *douar*.

Thus, too, a European of Algeria who has actively participated with his unit in the massacre of Algerians may, a few days later, be the victim of an attempt on his life organized by the *fidaïnes*.[10]

For the European population ignorant of the events that have determined the decision of the local cell of the F.L.N., the attempt may appear unjust and inexcusable. But for the other

[9] Jewish quarters of Moroccan towns.

[10] *fidaïnes*—plural of *fidaï*, a death volunteer, in the Islamic tradition.

members of the militia, who remember the cries of the men murdered in the *douar* and of the women being raped, the reason for this act is clear. The rightness of popular justice manifests itself in a particularly convincing way. The observer familiar with events in detail may notice in the course of the days following the attempt that several civil servants among the militiamen have asked for their transfer or else have literally fled to Algiers.

At other times, the Jews participate financially in the struggle and make a monthly contribution through an intermediary.

It is well for the French to know these things; as for the French authorities, they are well aware of them. It is well for the Jews to know them too, for it is not true that the Jew is in favor of colonialism and that the Algerian people reject him and relegate him to the camp of the oppressors.

The Algerian people, in truth, did not wait until 1959 to define their position with regard to the Jews. Here in fact is a passage from the appeal addressed in the form of a tract to the Jews of Algeria, at the most difficult moments of the Revolution, that is, in the fall of 1956:

> The Algerian people consider that it is their duty today to address themselves directly to the Jewish community in order to ask it solemnly to affirm its intention to belong to the Algerian Nation. This clearly affirmed choice will dissipate all misunderstandings and will root out the germs of the hatred maintained by French colonialism.

Already in the issue of the *Plate-forme* published in August 1956, the F.L.N. had declared, on the subject of the Jewish minority:

> Algerians of Jewish origin have not yet overcome their qualms of conscience, nor chosen sides.
>
> Let us hope they will, in great number, take the path of those who have responded to the call of the generous fatherland, and have given their friendship to the Revolution by already proudly proclaiming their Algerian nationality.

Jewish intellectuals have spontaneously demonstrated their support of the Algerian cause, whether in the democratic and traditionally anti-colonialist parties or in liberal groups. *Even today, the Jewish lawyers and doctors who in the camps or in prison share the fate of millions of Algerians attest to the multi-racial reality of the Algerian Nation.*

Various groups of the Jewish population of Algeria have likewise taken an official stand. In August 1956, a group of Jews in Constantine wrote:

> One of the most pernicious maneuvers of colonialism in Algeria was and remains the division between Jews and Moslems. . . . The Jews have been in Algeria for more than two thousand years; they are thus an integral part of the Algerian people. . . . Moslems and Jews, children of the same earth, must not fall into the trap of provocation. Rather, they must make a common front against it, not letting themselves be duped by those who, not so long ago, were offhandedly contemplating the total extermination of the Jews as a salutary step in the evolution of humanity.

In January 1957, in response to the Front's appeal, a group of Algerian Jews wrote:

> It is time, today, that we should return to the Algerian community. Attachment to an artificial French nationality is a snare and a delusion at a moment when the young and powerful modern Algerian nation is rapidly taking shape. . . . Jews have joined the ranks of the Algerians fighting for national independence. . . . Some have paid with their lives, others have bravely borne the foulest police brutalities, and many are today behind the doors of prisons and the gates of concentration camps. We also know that in the common fight Moslems and Jews have discovered themselves to be racial brothers, and that they feel a deep and lasting attachment to the Algerian fatherland. In proclaiming our attachment to the Algerian Nation, we put an end to the pretext used by the colonialists when they try to prolong their domination by making the French people believe that the revolt here is only the result of a medieval fanaticism. . . .

Algeria's Settlers

Another myth to be destroyed is that Algeria's settlers were unanimously opposed to the end of colonial domination.

Here again, French colonialism must know that the most important backing given by Algeria's Europeans to the people's struggle has been and remains that of the settlers. Even the

Algerians have been surprised by the frequency with which the settlers have responded to the appeals of the F.L.N. In any case, once contacted by the F.L.N., no settler has ever reported to the French authorities. It has happened that they have refused an appeal, but the secret has always been kept.

In the countryside, from the first months of 1955, the small settlers, the farmers, the managers were approached by turns. Of course, the known extreme rightists were systematically avoided. Generally speaking, especially in the small and medium population centers, men know one another, and the Algerian for his part has from the beginning put a label on every European. When an F.L.N. cell would decide to contact the Europeans in the region, the members knew at once who were the ones who should automatically be excluded. They also knew, though with less certainty, which ones would probably contribute their help to the Revolution.

Very often, especially in the small rural centers, only one member of the cell is made responsible for relations with the Europeans. One can readily imagine the vigilance that must be exercised in the first months of the struggle to prevent ill-advised moves on the part of militants not yet sufficiently disciplined. We have seen in fact that the European minority was seen as an undifferentiated whole within the framework of the colonial situation. On November 1, 1954, there was therefore an extreme oversimplification. The outlines and paradoxes of the world stood out in sudden sharpness.

The settler who helps the Revolution might be led to echo colonialist remarks in public—at the café or in a conversation—in order to assure the other Europeans of his solidarity. "With them the only thing that counts is force. . . . They're all in cahoots. . . ." The people, who have their ears to the ground, find out that these remarks have been made, and a new body of evidence builds up in the village. That settler is unanimously designated as a target for the *fadaïnes*. It then becomes necessary to intervene tactfully, to prohibit any act of hostility to the person or against the property of that settler and at the same time not give any hint as to the reasons for these instructions.

Sometimes it may be decided to burn a few haystacks in the fields of a settler who, in a region that has otherwise been razed to the ground by the F.L.N., has paradoxically suffered no damage. The colonialist Europeans sooner or later begin to wonder what is behind the Front's unusual respect for that settler's fields. We may mention also that in certain localities we have evidence of fires being set or livestock being slaughtered by European neighbors jealous of the protection a settler seems to enjoy, in contrast to the almost daily raids carried out by units of the A.L.N. on their properties.

Since 1955, many farms belonging to European settlers have been used by turns as infirmaries, refuges, or relay stations. When the French troops, in the course of their forays, began to make a habit of systematically destroying the grain reserves of the Algerian population, the A.L.N. decided to stock their supplies on the farms of Europeans. Thus several farms belonging to Europeans were transformed into A.L.N. granaries, and at nightfall sections of the A.L.N. units could be seen coming down from the mountains to take delivery of sacks of wheat or semolina.

At other times weapons would be stored on the farms. This was the period during which, in many areas, meetings would be held on European farms. Deliveries of arms were made under the sacred protection of the European settler. It sometimes happened, too, that settlers would accept the weapons that were delivered them by the French army—on the pretext of self-protection—and hand over to the A.L.N. those that they had had previously. Finally, since the beginning of the Revolution, a great number of European farmers have regularly been helping the Algerian Revolution financially.

The dozens of European settlers arrested for arms traffic, arms transport, financial support of "the rebellion," suffice to show the scope of this European participation in the national fight for liberation. The French authorities, since they have discovered this commitment of the Europeans to the cause of the Front, have formed the habit of keeping it hidden, or of branding these Europeans as Communists. This propaganda trick has two objectives: First, to revive the argument that North Africa is a target of Communist infiltration into the N.A.T.O. strategic system, into the heart of Western civilization. Next, to discredit those men, to present them as "foreign agents," even mercenaries. French colonialism refuses to admit that a genuine European can really fight side by side with the Algerian people.

European farmers, without engaging in combat, help the Front by refusing, for example, the protection that the French Army offers to provide them. These refusals are sometimes of consequence, for in farms happening to be in a crucial strategic area (a passageway between two mountains, frontier regions) the absence of colonial forces favors the movement of units of the A.L.N. or the supplying of the *moudjahidines*.[11] It sometimes happens that the French Army decides, in the course of a control operation in a given sector, to establish a post on a farm despite the settler's opposition. The owner then never fails to notify the Front that these quarters are being set up without his consent and that he has not asked anyone for protection.

The settler does his best, in fact, to make things uncomfortable for the French military, and in any case to communicate to the local chiefs of the F.L.N. detailed information as to the size and the morale of the unit posted on the farm.

Europeans in the Cities

In the urban centers Algeria's Europeans were to work essentially in the political cells. With the measures taken by the French ministers Soustelle and Lacoste, we found that pharmaceutical products and surgical instruments were hit by an embargo. We have already pointed out that directives addressed to doctors made it an obligation for them to notify the police authorities of any wounded man who appeared suspect.

[11] *Moudjahidines*—plural of *moudjahid*. Fighters (originally fighters in Moslem Holy War).

European doctors and pharmacists then began to treat wounded A.L.N. members without discrimination, and to deliver the antibiotics and the ether asked for by the F.L.N. militants. Hundreds of millions of units of penicillin daily made their way to the maquis.

Other doctors went further and unhesitatingly answered calls to go to the nearby mountains to treat the wounded. Sometimes when the wound was very serious the *moudjahid* would be taken in the doctor's car to a friendly clinic and treated for a week or two. The French police learned of these things, for after a certain period some of these clinics were regularly searched.

European nurses, for their part, found ways of spiriting surgical instruments, sulfa drugs, dressings from the hospitals.

It would also sometimes happen that, after a wounded prisoner had been operated on by French doctors, while still under the effect of anaesthesia he would disclose certain secrets. The nurse, after the wounded man was entirely awake, would advise him to be cautious and tell him what he had revealed. On the other hand, it could also happen that an intern present in the room would immediately telephone to the police who would then, two hours after a critical operation, subject the patient to real torture sessions.

European doctors likewise organized clandestine training courses for future medical corpsmen of the A.L.N. Several successive classes of medical corpsmen thus were turned out by these schools and joined those trained in corresponding centers directed by Algerian doctors.

European girls would put themselves at the disposal of a political cell, obtain paper and mimeograph machines, and would often handle the printing of F.L.N. tracts. Youngsters would make themselves responsible for driving members of a network in their cars. European families would take important political leaders under their wing and in a number of cases enabled them to escape General Massu's dragnets. European political figures, highly placed civil servants, furnished false passports, false identity cards, and false employment cards to F.L.N. cells.

It was thanks to the involvement of an increasingly large number of Algeria's Europeans that the revolutionary organization was able, in certain towns, to escape the police and the parachutists.

We know that many Europeans have been arrested and tortured for having sheltered and saved political or military leaders of the Revolution from the colonialist hounds.

The Europeans have not contented themselves with carrying medications and men in their cars. They also carry arms. Automatic pistols, cases of grenades, have thus been able to pass through all road-blocks, as Europeans are never searched carefully. It has even happened that, when a European's car has been searched, the driver, to avoid being molested, has explained the arms by saying he wanted to be ready to "smash the Arabs." Such an attitude delights the highway police, and this "anti-native" solidarity is frequently toasted in the nearest *bistro.*

Finally—and this is quite unexpected, though it has happened several times—members of the police will report to the local cell on planned operations, will warn a given Algerian that he is being watched or, at the last minute, advise him that a tortured prisoner has been made to talk and has named him as the local chief.[12]

Apart from the Europeans arrested and often frightfully tortured by the French troops for "complicity with the enemy" there are of course in Algeria a great number of Frenchmen engaged in the fight for liberation. Others have paid for their devotion to the Algerian national cause with their lives. It was thus, to give an example, that Maître Thuveny, an attorney of Oran, who had fought for a long time in the ranks of the F.L.N., died as the result of an assault organized in Morocco by the French Second Bureau.

[12] See Appendix II.

Appendix I[13]

The personal experience on which I am reporting—an Algerian European's awakening to a consciousness of his Algerian nationality—is in no way exceptional. Others have had it before me. It seems to me worth while, however, to show how European students without any past experience of political activity, having simply leftist leanings to begin with, have finally chosen in this war to be Algerians. Very few, to be sure, have carried their ideas through completely and joined the F.L.N. This must not be held against them. I know from experience how heart-rending this radical attitude can be. I should like simply to emphasize a fact too often overlooked: in the course of the Revolution, Europeans of Algeria have become conscious of belonging to the Algerian nation. While they are not a majority, they are nevertheless more numerous than is generally believed in Algeria or in the world. They cannot express themselves. It is in part in their name that I am speaking here.

When it broke out on November 1, 1954, the Algerian Revolution was suddenly to reveal our ambivalence. We had pronounced ourselves in favor of the right of the Vietnamese people and the Tunisian people to their independence. These positions were purely theoretical, however, as the total absence of political life in our community afforded no opportunity for concrete attitudes. As for the rights of the Algerian people, the question did not even arise, and we took refuge by comfortably and magically denying the problem. The segregation of political life into two "colleges" encouraged us in this: in the second college, the Algerian problems; in the first college, the French problems. So we would discuss and take positions on the C.E.D. and on the role of the French Communist Party in parliament.[14] Even the colonial problems were approached from a French point of view. This absence of curiosity with regard to our

[13] This appendix consists of the testimony of Charles Geromini, former intern at the Saint Anne Psychiatric Hospital in Paris.

[14] C.E.D.—The European Defense Community. See note 3, page 27 on the two-college system. (Translator's note)

country's burning problems had its origin, it must be recognized, in the unconscious race prejudice we all bore within us, having been inoculated by twenty years of colonial life. Being of the Left, we had, to be sure, surmounted the aggressive colonialist racism, but we had by no means rid ourselves of paternalism. Not the least of the shocks that we experienced was the realization that we were still racist in attitude.

From the very beginning, the colonialists would attack us, would ask us point-blank to choose, to be for or against the *fellagha,*[15] to be for France or "anti-France." In the beginning we still were bewitched. Refusing to take a position on the problem, we took refuge in protests against the brutalities of the repression. A committee of students for the defense of civil liberties had been set up. I decided to become a member. It was in this Committee that I was able for the first time to have political discussions with Algerians. Up to that time I had never had such conversations even with my best Moslem friends. A tacit agreement seemed to have been concluded; we recognized the validity of nationalist sentiments among our Moslem friends, but we never spoke of this so as not to break those bonds of friendship whose fragility we sensed. In this students' committee, relations between Moslems and ourselves were initially rather ambivalent. They wanted to give a political dimension to the committee's activity, while we felt it should remain on the humanitarian level. After we had passed a few motions condemning the repression, a concrete gesture was proposed to us. A student arrested in Paris had been transferred to Tizi-Ouzou. He had a clean record. It was decided that a delegation would go and bring him a parcel and deliver a letter of protest to the Attorney-General.

I volunteered. As the rule was to have equal representation of both national groups, the delegation included three Moslems and three Europeans: two Jews and myself. In the course of the trip, the conversation brought out many ideas shared by our

[15] *fellagha*—Algerian partisans.

Moslem comrades and ourselves: a common love of country, the same aspiration to transform it, to enrich it, the same desire to see it freed of all race prejudice, of any trace of colonialism. But we diverged on the question of the "rebellion." For my part, I considered it understandable, like an excess made possible by the excesses of colonialism, but I refused to accept the validity of violence. My Moslem comrades did not agree on this point, and we had a long discussion on the subject. They entirely approved of a profession of faith—patriotic, lyrical and passionate—that T——, a Jew, delivered to us in the course of a meal. I was greatly shaken by this profession of faith. It was undoubtedly what I needed to be moved to think about my relationship to the Algerian nation. I still had too much unconscious anti-Arab feeling in me to be convinced by a Moslem Arab. It took the speech by that Algerian Jew to shake me.

At Tizi-Ouzou we were barely allowed to get a glimpse of our comrade's lawyer. We were next called in by the police. We were questioned separately. At one point we saw a Moslem comrade coming out of the offices, very pale, supported by two police officers. We first thought he had been maltreated; but this was not the case. He had simply been threatened with reprisals to his family because of his brother in the maquis, who was being sought by the police. His name was Ben M'Hidi. His brother was Lardi Ben M'Hidi, in command of the *wilaya VI,* a member of the C.C.E.,[16] since then arrested and murdered by the French troops. I was the last to be questioned. The officer proceeded to lecture me: "You are the only Frenchman in the gang. . . ."

I broke in to remind him of the official position as formulated by the government: "Algeria is France, Algerians are Frenchmen."

"You are from France, of course."

"No, I was born in Algiers."

[16] *wilaya*—a military region (the Arab word for "province"). C.C.E.—Committee of Coordination and Execution. This was the body later succeeded by the F.L.N., that launched the insurrection. (Translator's note)

"Ah! So you don't know the real Arabs, who live in the villages."

"I have lived for eight years in Orléansville."

"Listen, you're young, you've let yourself be carried away. You'll understand later."

We were released only at about eight o'clock at night, after having been put through the criminal anthropometric department. To protest against this violation of rights, our student committee organized a public demonstration in a small hall. Three hundred students, nearly all Europeans, met under the chairmanship of two University professors. A resolution was passed condemning the excesses of the repression, demanding the restoration of democratic rights.

A few days later, with H——, I represented our committee at a meeting which was to organize a big protest gathering. For the first time I was put in contact with Moslem political leaders. These were M.T.L.D. town councillors. (See footnote 5, p. 148.) I was struck by their conscientiousness and their moderation. At the first meeting, discussions took place regarding the date of May 8th chosen for the meeting.[17] Although chosen solely for practical reasons, certain Europeans on the organizing committee felt that the choice of this anniversary might look like a deliberate provocation. The M.T.L.D. councillors agreed to a change of date, but H—— vehemently protested. They had not asked that the meeting be held on May 8th, but since some seemed to consider this anniversary as having a certain importance, he attached to it an even greater importance. "May 8th is a day of mourning for us, and we shall be telling the colonialists that we have not forgotten, that we shall never forget." These words somewhat shocked the Europeans, and there was a certain uneasiness, the Europeans refusing once again to look political reality in the face, and wanting to remain strictly within the limits of republican legality. In the end, the meeting was prohibited.

[17] May 8, 1945—the date of the Kabylian uprising in and around Sétif and Guelma.

Then, with the third quarter, came preparation for examinations; and the defense of democratic liberties was put on the back shelf. I continued to have discussions with my Moslem friends. Little by little, I was beginning to understand the meaning of the armed struggle and its necessity. But I expressed doubts as to the value of the armed action that was being carried on. Having no other source of information than the local press, we were subjected daily to the colonialist propaganda that made the *fellagha* out to be extremists and highway bandits. We partly accepted these views, but it could not be gainsaid that the horrors of the repression fully counterbalanced the "horrors" of the maquisards. Between the two we were looking for a third way out. I thought at the time that this was possible and that a liberal opinion was to be found in Algeria, capable of joining forces with French liberal opinion and of imposing a solution based on the recognition of the right of the people to make their own choices.

My discussions with members of my own family and with my friends became less and less frequent and were increasingly discouraging. Race prejudice had crystallized under the pressure of events, and it was impossible to get people to think dispassionately, to have an intellectual approach to the problem. A string of insults would quickly take the place of arguments: "Traitor—s.o.b.—pro-Arab—Communist—anti-French . . ." and especially the supreme insult, *"Mendessiste."* (I had never seen a man so hated as Mendès-France except Soustelle, a *"Mendessiste"* and a notorious Jew who betrayed France by wanting to give Algeria to the Arabs.)

But beneath these racialist outbursts it was easy to discern a deep anxiety: the fear of being run out of the country. "What will become of us?" was a question that often recurred when day-to-day events were discussed. Paralyzed by their anxiety, these Europeans could imagine no other solution than the perpetuation of the *status quo*. What Algeria's Frenchmen were most worried about, in fact, was whether or not they would be able to remain in Algeria. Having to leave—whether for France,

Canada or Brazil (as some were contemplating)—meant exile. I was able to calm people only by admitting that I shared their fears and that it was precisely in order to remain in Algeria that I was in favor of negotiation. "Let us frankly recognize," I said, "that Algeria is not France! Let us admit it openly since we all think it. You will grant that there have been political mistakes and social abuses in Algeria. Let us face it and let us discuss the future with the Algerians." I would be listened to with the pity bestowed on one who has lost his mind. The idea that one could come to terms with Arabs!

After endless discussions and mountains of reading, I began to see things more clearly. To fight for the humanization of the repression was futile! It was necessary to fight in order to impose a political solution. But *what* solution? It soon became clear to me that if even the embryo of a social revolution was to be created in Algeria, the colonial links with France would have to be broken. Algeria's very survival required that she promote the needed revolution, and this revolution could be accomplished only through independence. I had in this way come round to the ideals of the *fellagha!* Love of country, the passionate determination to live here, on the one hand, and on the other my revolutionary ideals, or more simply my leftist leanings, drove me toward the same goal as the Moslem nationalists. Yet I was too conscious of the different roads by which we had reached the same aspiration. Independence, yes. I agreed wholeheartedly. But *what* independence? Were we going to fight to build a theocratic, feudal, Moslem state that frowned on foreigners? Who could claim that we had a place in such an Algeria?

This was in July 1955, and until that day I had never read a single tract—a single tract emanating—from whom, indeed? People talked about the F.L.N., about the M.N.A.[18] The leaders of the former M.T.L.D. had been released, after being

[18] M.N.A.—*Mouvement Nationaliste Algérien,* a middle-of-the-road nationalist movement, whose leader was Messali Hadj, which refused to join forces with the F.L.N. (Translator's note)

arrested in November, because it was felt they were non-participants. Who was at the head of the Revolution? Apart from independence, what were the objectives of the revolutionaries? Was it a theocratic, a reformist, a democratic state that they were planning? T——told me, in answer, that this was certainly important but that in the last analysis it was up to the Algerian people themselves to decide; that one must be with the people, that this was the only way to transform the national revolution into a social revolution. T——, a member of the Algerian Communist Party, was sorry that his ideas were not shared by the Party, which was adopting a deplorable waiting policy. I saw a great deal of T——in the course of the summer of 1955, and we quickly agreed to work among the students. It appeared important to us to try to rally student liberal opinion at the reopening of the fall session and to launch a campaign of information to open the minds of the students to the idea of independence and of our integration into the Algerian nation. It was at this time that I saw the first tracts issued by the Front. I had previously been told of the democratic character it had acquired after the M.T.L.D. had split off from it. I must admit that these tracts were a relief to me: the future democratic and social state that they advocated was a cause for which it was possible to fight. The events of Philippeville of August 20 then broke out.[19] I attached a good deal of importance to them and I firmly condemned them, but they did not shake my determination to help the Revolution.

The dissolution of the Algerian Communist Party, the ever greater restrictions on civil liberties, the growing irritation of the Europeans, the rise of fascism that we could observe among our student comrades, confirmed us in our ideas. It was necessary to create a solid leftist force in the University, which would be capable of resisting the fascist upsurge, to bring out an information bulletin which would open the eyes of the European students to begin with, and have an impact on at least a part of

[19] August 20, 1955—an uprising in the course of which many whites were massacred. (Translator's note)

the community. Ambitious though it was, this program was not misdirected, as was shown by the importance that the fascist students assumed on February 6th and May 13th. Unfortunately, we were unable to carry it through.

Within the framework of this plan we made contact with the various student factions. T——asked me if I would agree to meet some nationalist students of "F.L.N. tendencies." I was of course willing, and one day we met a medical student, L. Khène,[20] at the El Kattar hospital. The meeting was very cordial. Khène was sceptical as to the results, but he was willing to participate in the first meetings. I next made contact with students who had formed an association under the convenient label of "progressive and Mandouzist."[21] C——, one of the outstanding members, showed no enthusiasm and refused on various pretexts to participate. T——and I quickly got the impression that C——had something better to do than to play with students.

After two or three meetings, nothing came of our group except a few motions that we were unable either to distribute or to have printed in the newspapers. The hope of launching a bulletin and of broadcasting our ideas among the students quickly evaporated. It was then decided to amend our plans. We set up a study group that was to deal with certain economic questions. Wanting to be Algerians, we felt it was obviously the duty of all of us either to betake ourselves to the maquis, or else seriously to prepare ourselves to become the country's future leaders in the professional and technical fields. Our qualifications as fighters were more than dubious, and as we were not heroes, wisdom easily prevailed. But we were ready to help the Front if it were to call upon us.

Meanwhile the atmosphere in Algeria was becoming increasingly charged. Morocco's accession to independence and the dissolution of the National Assembly gave rise to an agitation that

[20] Lamine Khène. Since then, Secretary of State in the Provisional Government of the Algerian Republic.

[21] Mandouze, a liberal Catholic professor, detested by the settlers. (Translator's note)

kept mounting until the outbreak on February 6th.[22] We became more and more known and we were sometimes insulted in the street by people we did not know. On the other hand, "liberal" students increasingly came to ask us to explain things, wanting to be told about the Revolution, concerned over the future of the country and asking to have contact with Moslem students. With the latter and with the U.G.E.M.A.[23] we had frank and open relations, devoid of any misunderstanding. They considered us Algerians. Common activities, even minor ones—mimeographing and distributing together the tracts of the U.G.E.M.A., assuring orderliness during conferences—made us more readily accepted. But the wall of distrust was sometimes slow to vanish.

On the occasion of elections to the Students' General Assembly, our small group was able to draw up so-called liberal lists in nearly all the schools to oppose the fascist lists. Aided by the blundering racism of our adversaries and by effective work among the Jewish minority, an effective wave of anti-racism developed. For the first time in its history, the elected General Assembly was a left-wing one, ready to follow the recommendations of the U.N.E.F.[24] against tortures and violations of legality. This quickly became clear when three students were arrested. With Ben Yahia and Ben Batouche we drafted a motion demanding that the legal time limit of incarceration in police headquarters be respected, and warning against physical maltreatment.[25] This motion, unanimously adopted, created a certain stir among the students. But the results of the elections to

[22] February 6, 1956—Departure of Soustelle from Algiers and arrival of Guy Mollet, then the new French Prime Minister, which set off the first major settlers' demonstration, in the course of which the Premier was pelted with tomatoes and other objects and frightened into abandoning the moderate policy he had come to initiate. (Translator's note)

[23] U.G.E.M.A.—*Union Générale des Etudiants Musulmans Algériens.*

[24] U.N.E.F.—*Union Nationale des Etudiants Français,* a progressive student organization with nation-wide membership in France.

[25] Ben Yahia, the president of the General Union of Algerian Students, who later became a member of the National Council of the Algerian Revolution. Ben Batouche, commander of the Army of National Liberation, who was later killed in battle.

the French National Assembly soon came and swept other concerns into the background. How close we then seemed to our goal! The triumph of the Left in France justified all our hopes. Anxious students kept coming to us in increasing number. "What is going to become of us when negotiations begin and Algeria, perhaps, acquires her independence? Will we still be able to remain?" It then occurred to us to organize meetings of Moslem students and European students. Two or three such meetings took place where everyone spoke freely. The Europeans' worries were expressed mainly in aggressive terms: respect for the rights of the minority, respect for culture, for religion. On every point the Moslems gave their reply. And as in a psychodrama, the aggressiveness would disappear with the anxiety. I was able to observe that this easing of tension occurred when the Moslems declared: "You are Algerians, just as we are, but if you want to leave the country you are free to do so." And the Europeans would always answer, "We don't want to leave and we don't want to be strangers in this country." On such a basis fruitful discussions could take place.

Meanwhile February 6th was approaching. The atmosphere had become nervous, tense, irritating. We received threatening letters and insulting telephone calls.

The fascists made their first attempt on the deputy Hernu. Then it was Camus's turn.[26] We had gone to his lecture to hear one of our elders and if need be protect him from the fascists. On this point we were not called on to intervene. Camus's audience had been carefully screened and the approaches to the hall were guarded by the helmeted C.R.S.[27] We expected that Camus would take a clear postion on the Algerian problem. What we were treated to was a sweet-sister speech. He explained to us at length that the innocent civilian population must be protected, but he was categorically against fund raising in favor of the innocent families of political prisoners. We in the hall

[26] Hernu—a radical-socialist of the Mendès-France persuasion. Albert Camus—the Algerian-born French writer, Nobel prize-winner in 1957.

[27] C.R.S.—*Compagnie Républicaine de Sécurité,* a national constabulary army corps, independent of the regular army. (Translator's note)

were dumbfounded. Outside, the mob of fascists was rhythmically yelling: *"Algérie française!"* and screaming: "Camus to the gallows!"

But these demonstrations seemed to us to be the dying spasms of the colonialist beast. Even the monster-demonstration on the occasion of Soustelle's departure, even Professor Bousquet's hysterical appeals and their repercussions among the students did not faze us. We had an immense hope in the new French government invested by the entire Assembly to make the peace. Not for a moment did we doubt that this government would put an end to fascism in Algeria. What Edgar Faure and his majority of the center had done in Morocco, Guy Mollet and his left-wing majority would surely do more easily in Algiers. When I say "we," I am not only speaking of the Europeans. I am also thinking of the Moslems who thought as we did that the end was near and who were asking us to work together in the imminent peace as we had done in the war.

Then came February 6th. For two days the whole city had been a seething cauldron of excitement. Columns paraded through the streets waving the *tricolore* and singing the *Marseillaise,* shouting: *"Algérie française!"* Cars wove back and forth, tossing out tracts, honking without let-up. Such was the atmosphere in which Guy Mollet was received. I was not present at the scene of the monument honoring the dead, but my comrades told me about it. Not for a moment had we thought that this welcome could make Guy Mollet come to the grave decisions that followed. We thought, on the contrary, that, irritated by Algeria's Europeans, he would have fewer scruples, a less uneasy conscience about imposing the negotiated solution that we were all looking forward to. And so we were stupefied to learn at the end of the afternoon of General Catroux's resignation. It was Ben Batouche who announced it to us. He was overwhelmed. I saw Khène, next to me, turn pale and clench his fists with fury. All around us people were embracing amid great bursts of laughter, singing the *Marseillaise.* The city suddenly took on the appearance of a vast fair. I was nauseated by so much stupidity. As we separated, one of us said, "And now we have no one left but the F.L.N. to speak for us." It quickly became obvious to us that with France reluctant to make the fascist minority of Algeria toe the mark, it was henceforth up to the F.L.N. to do so. After February 6th we could no longer turn our eyes toward France. Not from her would salvation come. The extraordinary apathy of the French people, confirmed in the course of a trip I took to Paris, convinced me of this.

In the face of the fascist-Lacoste surge our group disintegrated. What, after all could we do? There was no longer any choice other than between Lacoste and the Front. A third force could have had meaning only if it had been supported by the French Left. Since the French Left was playing the game of Algerian fascism, any attempt to organize liberal action in Algiers was doomed to failure. No one among us had any illusions as to this. And in fact the subsequent so-called liberal movement was in large part composed of metropolitan civil servants on duty in Algeria.

Our Moslem comrades were soon to join the maquis, and the Communists, after the Maillot case, turned to clandestine action.[28] The others performed some minor services on the spot: acting as letter-boxes, providing shelter, etc. I had left Algiers for the psychiatric hospital in Blida, which had the reputation of being a nest of *fellagha.* As an intern with a doctor known for his anti-colonialist views, I was soon classified, rejected by some and adopted by others. I remained for eight months in Blida, wholly absorbed in my work as an intern. My solidarity with the Revolution was limited to helping distribute tracts, and passing around copies of *El Moudjahid* that I had in my possession. I had agreed to do medical work, but the opportunity to commit myself further never materialized. In late December 1956 I left Blida for Paris. A whole set of arguments accounted for this departure, or this disguised flight. Apart from

[28] Maillot—a young French Algerian non-commissioned officer, a Communist, who dynamited an electric tower and was guillotined.

family reasons, I especially needed perspective. As I was not working for the Front, I realized my uselessness. Besides, the birth of terrorism in the city revived problems of conscience which the super-tense atmosphere of Algeria made impossible to resolve with a cool head. Finally, my wife's (ill-founded) fear of my being arrested (although arbitrary arrests were daily occurrences) was without doubt the decisive argument.

In France I thought I would find rest. I found only a bad conscience. Every day the newspapers brought news of arrests and of firings of friends of mine. Every fresh item of news depressed me more. I felt even more useless. I tried to fight, to stir up reactions of protest among those around me, to make them understand. It was wasted effort. The Parisians had their minds only on their evenings out, on the plays they wanted to see, on their vacations that had to be planned three months ahead of time. I found myself detesting them, despising all those Frenchmen who sent their sons off to torture people in Algeria and cared about nothing but their little shops. I rejected any feeling I had about belonging to the French nation. My people were certainly not those bourgeois devoid of any ideal. They were the people who suffered and died every day in the *djebels* and in the torture chambers.

These initial reactions, to be sure, became attenuated. I developed sound friendships with democratic fellow interns for whom this colonial war waged by their country was a cause of deep suffering. But I felt at home only with Algerian émigrés.

This stay in France turned out in the end to be very profitable. It confirmed for me what I already sensed: that I was not French, that I had never been French. Language, culture—these are not enough to make you belong to a people. Something more is needed: a common life, common experiences and memories, common aims. All this I lacked in France. My stay in France showed me that I belonged to an Algerian community, showed me that I was a stranger in France.

When my draft exemption expired in May 1958, I did not hesitate long. I had already decided to join the F.L.N.

It is a year now since I have joined the Algerian Revolution. Remembering the difficult and ambiguous contacts I had had at the outset of the Revolution, I had some fear that I might not be welcomed. My fear was unfounded. I was welcomed like any other Algerian. For the Algerians I am no longer an ally. I am a brother, simply a brother, like the others.

Appendix II

My name is Bresson Yvon. After having spent my entire youth in Algeria, in Bone, I went to France in 1948 to continue my studies there.

In 1952, after my military service, I took the competitive examination for a commission in the Algerian police. I was admitted and assigned to the *Sécurité Publique* of Saint-Arnaud, a large village of the Upper Constantine Plateaux, some thirty kilometers from Sétif. On May 6, 1953, I took over my post as police officer. I was then twenty-four years old.

It must be remembered that Saint-Arnaud is located at the center of the region of Sétif, where in 1945 more than 40,000 Algerians were massacred in three days. The Europeans for whose protection I was responsible were the very ones who, ten years before, had participated in the *Arab hunt.* These men were still reminiscing about their exploits in 1953 and comparing their respective records. I had very few private dealings with these Europeans in Saint-Arnaud. On the other hand, I established friendships with Algerians and even with a number of known nationalists. My superiors, superintendents Gavini Antoine and Lambert Marius, of course warned me. The most excited European civilians, whenever the occasion arose, kept reminding me of *the rule:* to keep the Arabs down.

On November 1, 1954, the Revolution broke out.

Very quickly I came to realize that I belonged in the camp of those who fight for an Algerian nation. The countless tortures that I had occasion to witness in the exercise of my duties were to strengthen my hatred of colonialism: Algerians torn apart by two military trucks driven in opposite directions, classic tortures by water, electricity, hanging by the thumbs or by the testicles.

One day my wife who had been kept awake all night, as she had for several weeks, by the cries of the tortured (we lived above one of the torture chambers of Saint-Arnaud), unable to stand it any longer, went and violently protested to the soldiers and the C.R.S. responsible for these practices. She was led back to the house with two machine guns digging into her ribs. It was at this period that I was contacted by a member of the local F.L.N. cell. To this cell I was to communicate various items of information useful for the carrying on of the national war of liberation.

I was able to pass on word as to the hour and place of round-ups, as to which Algerians were being followed, as to which cafés were suspected. I passed on the entire secret report addressed by Superintendent Gavini to the Sub-Prefect of Sétif regarding the impending internment of Dr. Lamine Debaghine, the present Minister of Foreign Affairs of the Provisional Government of the Algerian Republic.

I had occasion to give the names of Algerian informers employed by the colonialist police. These agents were obviously very dangerous, for they sometimes managed to find out a considerable number of secrets.

In May 1956, Hamou Abdallah, a veteran who ran a Moorish café, one of the most active secret agents, was executed in the middle of the rue Saint-Augustin. A few months later another spy, Aktouf Mustapha, was in turn grievously wounded.

In June 1956, Superintendent Gavini, exhausted by several months of torture sessions, left on sick leave. I was then put in charge of the *Commissariat*. In the archives I got hold of a list of names of Algerian suspects who were recommended to be executed in short order. This list was the work of my colleague Sphonix Jean and of Second Lieutenant Varini Camille.

I made a copy of it, which I immediately passed on to the local chief. Shortly after this I was arrested. Before this, however, I was able to communicate to the chief an inventory of the weapons supplies and ammunition reserves in certain posts.

The Political Superintendent of the Southern Zone (the Northern and Southern Zones were separated by the national highway that divided the village in two) decided on the basis of this information to attack several farms and to destroy a number of French Army outposts.

Before my arrest, on the occasion of the murder of Ben Mihoud Saïd, a burst of machine gun bullets was fired in my direction. I was not hit.[29]

Summary executions increased in number under the direction of Major Puech. Thus, to give an example, fifty Algerians were executed and buried in a plot belonging to the Mayor of Saint-Arnaud.

On November 18, 1956, I was arrested by order of General Dufour and brought before the military tribunal which condemned me to five years' imprisonment with a suspended sentence.

It is as an Algerian that I have done all these things. I do not have the impression of having betrayed France. I am an Algerian, and like any Algerian I have fought and I continue to fight colonialism. As a conscious Algerian citizen, I felt I must take my place by the side of the patriots. This is what I have done.

[29] Ben Mihoud Saïd, public scribe, was killed by militia-men, on September 26, 1956. He was on the list of suspects to be executed by the government forces.

Conclusion

We have tried in the preceding pages to shed light on a few aspects of the Algerian Revolution. The originality and the impatient richness of the Revolution are now and forever the great victories of the Algerian people. This community in action, renovated and free of any psychological, emotional, or legal subjection, is prepared today to assume modern and democratic responsibilities of exceptional moment.

The thesis that the launching of a new society is possible only within the framework of national independence here finds its corollary. The same time that the colonized man braces himself to reject oppression, a radical transformation takes place within him which makes any attempt to maintain the colonial system impossible and shocking. It is this transformation that we have studied here.

It is true that independence produces the spiritual and material conditions for the reconversion of man. But it is also the inner mutation, the renewal of the social and family structures that impose with the rigor of a law the emergence of the Nation and the growth of its sovereignty.

We say firmly that Algerian man and Algerian society have stripped themselves of the mental sedimentation and of the emotional and intellectual handicaps which resulted from 130 years of oppression. This same colonialism that held the people in the tight meshes of the police and of the army is today wounded to the death. French colonialism in Algeria has always developed on the assumption that it would last forever. The structures built, the port facilities, the airdromes, the prohibition of the Arab language, often gave the impression that the enemy committed himself, compromised himself, half lost himself in his prey, precisely in order to make any future break, any separation, impossible. Every manifestation of the French presence expressed a continuous rooting in time and in the Algerian future, and could always be read as a token of an indefinite oppression.

It was the size of the European settlement, the rapacity of the settlers and their racist philosophy that required of every French expression in Algeria a maximum of solidity and of weight. Likewise, it was the robustness and the vehemence of French achievements that maintained and reinforced the oppressive category of colonialism.

To the history of the colonization the Algerian people today oppose the history of the national liberation.

It remains to be seen whether the French government will become aware of what is still possible. We have reviewed the victorious progress of the colonized on the path of his liberation, as revealed in a number of its particular aspects. We have indicated that strictly on the level of the individual and his tremendous dynamism a revolution—fundamental, irreversible, ever more far-reaching—has occurred.

It is now time for reason to make itself heard. If the French Government now hopes to revive the conditions that existed before 1954 or even 1958, it is well that it should know that this is now impossible. If on the other hand, it is willing to take account of the changes that have occurred in the consciousness of Algerian man in the last five years, if it is willing to lend an ear to the insistent and fraternal voices that give impetus to the Revolution and that are to be heard in the struggle of a people who spare neither their blood nor their suffering for the triumph of freedom, then we say that everything is still possible.

The crushing of the Algerian Revolution, its isolation, its

asphyxiation, its death through exhaustion—these are mad dreams.

The Revolution in depth, the true one, precisely because it changes man and renews society, has reached an advanced stage. This oxygen which creates and shapes a new humanity—this, too, is the Algerian Revolution.